NORTH
LIGHT
Collection

2

North Light Publishers

WESTPORT, CONN. 06880

NORTH LIGHT Collection

2

....the works, viewpoints and techniques of contemporary artists as featured in the pages of NORTH LIGHT magazine

Edited by

Walt Reed

Published by NORTH LIGHT PUBLISHERS, a division of
FLETCHER ART SERVICES, INC., 37 Franklin Street,
Westport, Conn. 06880.

Distributed to the trade by Van Nostrand Reinhold Company,
a division of Litton Educational Publishing, Inc.
450 W. 33rd Street, New York, N.Y. 10001

Manufactured in U.S.A.
First Printing 1979

Library of Congress Cataloging in Publication Data
Main entry under title:

North Light Collection 2.

   1. Art, American.
   2. Art, Modern — 20th Century — United States.
   I. Reed, Walt. II. North Light.
N6512.N625 709'.73 79-4615
ISBN 0-89134-016-5

Printed and bound by Kingsport Press.

NORMAN ROCKWELL (1894-1978)   PABLO PICASSO (1881-1973)

Perhaps no two artists were better known during their lifetimes.

Yet they could not have been further apart in their approach to picture making, nor more the subject of controversial critical opinion. Most people loved one and hated the other.

Rockwell, a traditional realist, presented us with an idealized version of ourselves as we wanted to be. His *Four Freedoms* gave tangible aims for America during World War II.

Picasso smashed and reassembled old art traditions in a major series of revolutionary pictures. *Guernica* is one of the strongest anti-war paintings ever made.

However their relative artistic merit will be assessed by posterity, they were alike in their dedication to their work and to their personal beliefs and this book is dedicated to their two great artistic talents.

The first NORTH LIGHT COLLECTION, published in 1972, has gone out of print, but the success of that first volume has encouraged the publication of NORTH LIGHT COLLECTION 2.

In the interim, the pages of NORTH LIGHT MAGAZINE have continued to provide a showcase for the work of many of America's most talented artists. And, as a source book for artists, editorial stress has always been placed on the artist's thinking and working methods, for the edification of other artists and for students of art.

Readers will find, therefore, that this new compilation from past issues of NORTH LIGHT MAGAZINE will offer a valuable descriptive selection of various points of view and methods of working which can serve as an inspirational and educational guide.

CONTENTS:

...a source book for artists

North Light

Bill Joli

hile **preparing** for this article, staring at the wall and reviewing how I work (write a two minute speech on how to tie shoelaces) I found that I do not have a set approach. When involved in a new assignment I may not remember all the procedures of the previous one. For me, there are periods in almost every job that are absorbing — when the work jells and my relationship to it seems intimate, deft and spontaneous. I wish it were true that such feelings result in a good job but it isn't always true. Sometimes I don't know if I've done a good job or if I'll like it tomorrow. We work mostly for feeling and any part, or all, of a lesser process which impedes feeling should be discarded. This includes nomenclature, work itineraries and the hourly rate.

It has been said that "a painting is never finished, it is only abandoned". If this be true in illustration, every client receives a job which fully satisfies only the deadline.

With the awareness that I don't quite know what I'm doing and that I have a deadline for this article, let's push on.

For me a felt sculpture is a paper sculpture with a felt face. The felt is laminated onto a white bond paper. One-coat rubber cement is applied to both the felt and the paper. When dry the pieces are joined and pressed firmly together by pulling a straight edge, across the felt. Tracing paper is used to protect the felt.

Later, when shapes are cut from the paper-cement-felt sandwich, the white bond will show, unwanted, along every edge. However, color markers match the stock colors of felt and when applied to the paper side of the sandwich the color will bleed through and color the other side of the porous paper with little risk of staining the felt. From the felt side the paper backing becomes invisible.

Shapes cannot be traced directly on the felt without soiling it but they can be reversed and traced onto the paper. The traced lines are easily seen and alterations can be drawn on the paper before the shape is cut. The paper is heavy ledger bond. The felt is Central Shippee Show Felt which is available in eighty stock colors.

The sketch for a felt bas relief must be done with the finished 3D forms in mind. About half of my commercial assignments are in two dimensional illustration, and I frequently draw shapes and convolutions of shapes in a sketch for a sculpture which the medium "will not allow". This is desirable — it helps to keep me vulnerable. I try to draw for color (the volumes and kinds of colors the shapes will contribute to the finish) for roughness or smoothness (the surface feel which the photo will, hopefully, catch) and for compositional passages (congestions of forms, simple tracts, emptiness, etc.).

In a sketch for a paper sculpture I sometimes try to draw for the highlight which each form will produce. In a curved form the highlight can be made to occur anywhere on the surface along the axis of the curve. A fast curve gives a sharp narrow reflection and a slow gentle curve gives a broad hazy one. These straight reflections in combination provide abstract phrases which add interest to the subject and freedom from the dark sides of forms and can be considered as a liet motif within the value patterns.

In a felt sculpture the reflections are very subtle because of the texture. In drawing for it I may try for tactile transitions between light and dark areas and linear movements derived from the thickness of the felt. Felt tends to look rougher in a photo than it does to the eye because each fibre takes light as if it were a fine wire. A light even enough to avoid this effect will flatten the bas relief.

Or, I may try for nothing more than a nice drawing and leave these and other considerations for the finish.

In submitting a sketch for a sculpture I ask that it be approved mostly for size, subject and style as the finish may not follow any other indication. I try not to do color sketches because they can not be duplicated in relief and they take too long. Colors in the "flat" do not relate to each other as colors in the "round" do. It is

RAY AMEIJIDE
The Rainbow Snipper

His name comes from Galicia in northern Spain. He comes from Newark in New Jersey.

His ability started to show in high school where he was awarded a St. Gaudens Medal.

After the war he graduated *twice* from Pratt Institute — which is two times more than some and once more than most.

After a two year wife-approved sabbatical to "follow his inclinations" he became resident illustrator for 5 years in a commercial New York studio.

He did his first paper sculpture during a lull — there have been very few lulls since.

You'll see why.

better to react freely to the sculpture as it grows than to be constrained by a prophecy.

This sketch is for the client; if he approves it, I do a work sketch for me. In it I try to delineate the style and its shapes as tightly as I can with a Mongol #2 pencil on tracing paper to the size I want the finish to be. The drawing is spray fixed and its face is covered with a light blue pastel rubbed in to remove excess powder.

At this point the felt colors are selected and assigned to shapes. The selection will change as the sculpture develops and makes its own demands. Flesh tones are good to start with, then large items of clothing. Background colors can wait.

The shapes cannot be traced along the lines of the drawing. They must be distorted so that, when formed, their outlines will correspond to the lines of the sketch. The tracing line enlarges that shape at right angles to the axis of the intended curve or bend. I guess as to the enlargement needed; if the piece is wrong, I use it as a guide toward a correct piece.

The drawing is reversed with its blue pastel face placed against the white paper side of the felt sandwich. The distorted shape to be cut is drawn around its equivalent in the sketch with a 6H pencil which transfers it, via the pastel, on to the bond paper. A shape which is partly covered in the sketch must be drawn to include the

covered area. A leg, for instance, can be drawn up to the navel even though it will be covered by a coat. This allows for hidden glue points. The 6H pencil leaves a light thin line on the drawing and, even if the sheet becomes crowded with 6H lines, the master drawing will still show. The distasteful alternative to this single sheet process is to draw all shapes separately on a lot of sheets.

The piece is cut with whatever type or size of scissors seems suitable. Its paper back is colored with the appropriate marker, it is formed by curling it against a smooth round dowel, brush or rod, and glued into position on the sculpture with either Duco or UHU cement. It is held in place until the glue sets. If the piece is to be scored, the score line is drawn on the paper side with a little more pressure on the 6H pencil, to indent the paper, and formed.

If the form itself does not provide adequate, hidden, glue points or proper elevation from other forms, Strathmore 2 ply tabs are added to the back. Often a piece will have 2 or 3 supports behind it. And so, little by little, in a process similar to plumbing, the sculpture grows. One bas relief (foolishly) had some 2400 visible pieces.

During assembly the sculpture is constantly checked against a predetermined light source because the finished art is not the sculpture but a photograph of it. Matt Sultan, the photographer for most of my

sculpture, and I have settled on a single strobe with umbrella at somewhere between 9 and 11 o'clock as our standard set up. If experiments with other lighting seem better we drop the standard.

This procedural tedium is often enlivened by welcome forces. As the sculpture grows, your relationship to it changes. You like it more or less or don't care. It begins to oppose the intentions of your sketch. It gets bigger (so far none have become smaller). It wants extra forms. It needs more time. It demands a new drawing. It finds your wife intrusive.

In the end you are both mugged by the deadline.

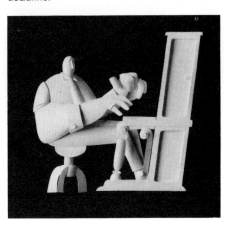

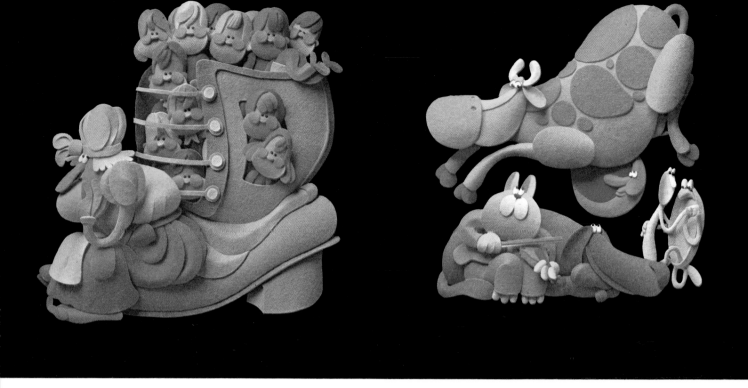

MOTHER GOOSE SERIES

These four were part of a series based on Mother Goose rhymes with the rhyme printing in the upper left corner of each panel. The originals were to be in a traveling display for a year; and, for fear that the paper-rubber-cement-felt laminate might not hold up, I glued each piece along its rim with UHU cement.

The black background was chosen because it eliminates the scattered and disturbing cast shadows that would show on a white field, and thus, allows for more complex forms in the sculpture. Its neutrality also tends to unify story content. They were photographed against an out of focus black velvet.

PIANO PLAYER (P. 11)

This was part of a series on musicians for one color reproduction. In a white on white sculpture the photographer has only shadows to work with (there is no variety of local color) and those shadows, irrespective of subject, should be interesting in the abstract. Large simple forms are less confusing than intricate detailing. I tried to play the soft gentle curves against the hard paper edges. The sculpture was made of 3 ply Strathmore to hold the gentle curves and yet be rigid enough not to need supports which in a white sculpture might be seen through a thinner stock.

Courtesy RCA Victor

The assignment here was to show a variety of family members receiving the client's product for Christmas. The logo appeared on the box. Because of space limitations the overall proportions had to be strictly maintained. I cut flat shapes for each figure, a little smaller than each would be in 3D, and the figures were assembled on them. The couch was constructed last to accommodate the figures. Intertwined figures, such as the couple necking, were considered as single units.

THE FRONT COVER

This was one of a series of ten illustrations for a humorous history of the world — and my first felt sculptures. My general technique developed during this construction.

This piece (a take-off on Da Vinci's helicopter) was an attempt to use felt on a free standing structure. It is not a true model since the forms are distorted to "read" from one side only and the depth was kept to about 3 inches to avoid depth of field problems in its photography.

The copter's frame is made of wire with strips of felt over it, like sleeves with the glued seam on the back. The screw required two pieces of felt, as it turns back on itself, and its outside curve was cut after the sections were assembled.

Courtesy Esso Research & Engineering Co.

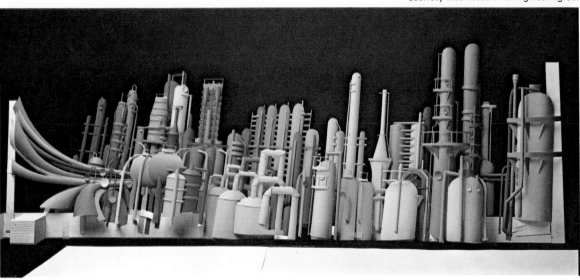

In this piece I was given free interpretive rein except that the individual refinery structures were to remain recognizable. The slant was chosen to lend sweep to an essentially vertical and linear subject and to place each cylindrical form at almost right angles to the light source, and so contain the cast shadows of the horizontal elements. It was assembled, unit by unit, on a penciled grid (later removed) with a strip of illustration board at its base on which the units were glued. The art was cropped in reproduction so none of the "behind-the-scenes" construction showed as it does here. I used paper and cardboard struts throughout for positioning and rigidity.

13

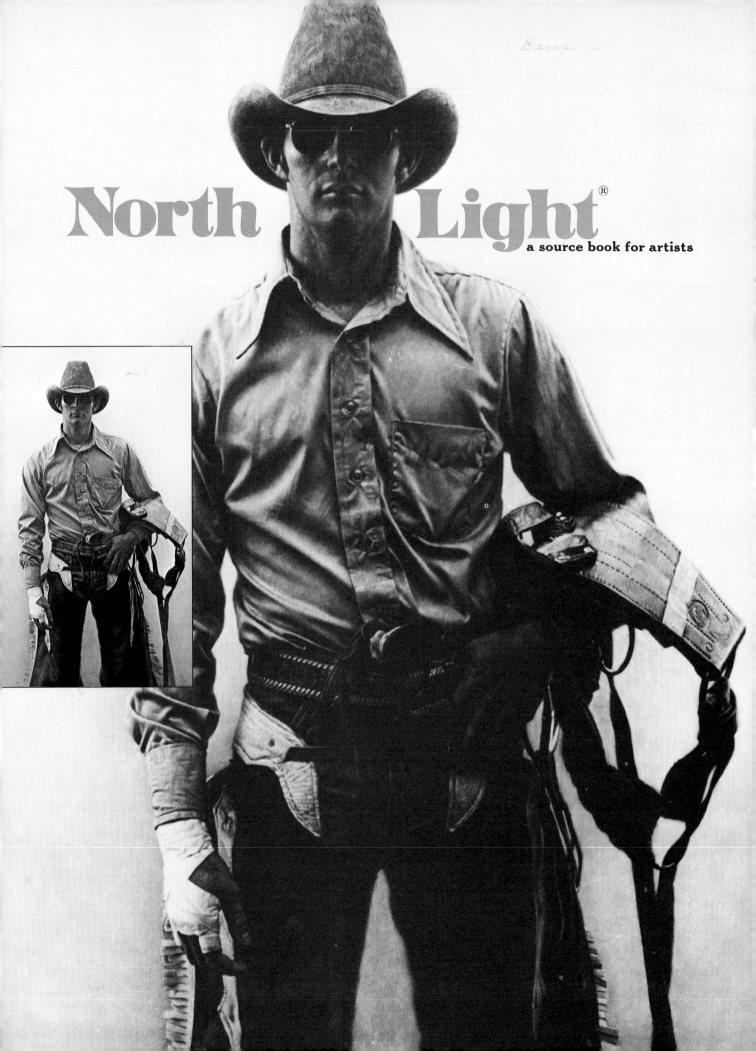

North Light®

a source book for artists

JIM BAMA...

THE CHALLENGE FOR AN ARTIST of putting his thoughts and ideas into written form is formidable indeed. But after 24 years of painting perhaps it is time to step back and reflect. If anyone had suggested 7 years ago that I would be living in Wyoming and "retired" as an illustrator and painting for myself, I would have questioned their sanity.

Having been born in New York City, and gone to high school and art school and been an illustrator there for many years, I felt firmly entrenched. The advance of photography and fast film actually accelerated my commercial career when big-time illustration began to stagger. Many situations could not be photographed, yet the realistic effect was desired, and my style lent itself to this need.

But I had seen too many contemporaries leveled by the fads of editorial work and advertising and the need for constant change. Also, one begins to question life and its goals in one's 40's. When do you begin to do what you want and produce work up to your own highest standards?

A chance vacation to Wyoming in 1966 to former illustrator Bob Meyers' guest ranch first planted the western seed. A second visit the following year made my wife and me realize that perhaps there was a better life than that in New York — surely a more challenging one. It took another year of planning before we left New York in our truck, with most of our books and furniture in storage.

After 42 years in New York City, the first challenge was in adjusting to life on a ranch 36 miles from the nearest town. It also required a tremendous amount of inner drive and physical vitality to go on working without the deadlines I had been accustomed to for years. I painted days, with no thought of selling, only trying to do the best paintings possible. I spent as long as five and a half months on one painting. I lived a double life, since I was still doing illustration at night. Up to this time illustration had been my *whole* life, but now I began to resent its intrusion on my time.

After two and a half years, paintings had begun to

a young man who **did** go West

The paintings shown here are from Bama's recent smash show at the prestigious Hammer Galleries on New York's 57th Street.

Viewers didn't just look at these works — they *peered* as closely as the length of their noses permitted!

Come closer. See for yourself . . . a remarkable hand — belonging to a young man who is just now beginning to realize his enormous potential.

TONY MARTIN — a nice young fellow who rode by my house during bear hunting season in the mist and rain in this wonderful poncho slicker. One of a breed of young guys who just wants to be a cowboy.

This is CHESTER MEDICINE CROW with his father's flag.

accumulate, and the time had come to take the plunge. I had never tried to sell a painting before. When we arrived back in New York in May, 1971, I had 18 framed paintings. I went to my only appointment at a gallery feeling like a student right out of art school. The thought of crating the paintings and sending them back to Wyoming or storing them in New York gave me a desperate courage, and all went well. The first day one was hung it was sold. I was now a "fine artist"! After about 13 sales in several months I left illustration for good.

I had never thought of being a "western artist" and still don't consider myself one. But what a wonderful source of inspiration and material I have found to say what I wanted to say about life and work and what I believe in. Out here you see the remains of the early settlers; their cabins, saddles, and other artifacts. There are people still living that are older than the state of Wyoming. One is made more aware of the sad fate of the Indians, and of the changes that are taking place out here even now: the developers and retired easterners, the tourist business, and

other forms of "progress". The rape of the old West is here, but there is still a chance to capture some of what once was.

I have met Indians one generation removed from famous fighting chiefs, prospectors, mountain men, rodeo performers, former stage coach drivers, homesteaders who came out in covered wagons, hunting guides and outfitters. I have tried to approach all this with a fresh eye. What excites me is sometimes taken for granted by artists who were born in the West. Also, the many years of illustration gives one a broad background and a greater range in solving a given problem. On the other hand, it's very difficult to avoid being anecdotal after doing so much editorial work. I try to do only controlled situations, and generally avoid action paintings.

The constant challenge is to keep growing and not to succumb to any temporary success. That, I feel, is an artist's true security. If you please yourself, you usually please others. May this article serve as a possible inspiration to other artists and old friends.

This is a buffalo skull that was an Indian kill and makes a great bullseye. The stone was the type used to do this.

OLD SADDLE IN SNOW — A 100 year old saddle I acquired. Set it out in the snow and waited several weeks. The night the snow fell just right, the temperature was —20°. Took pictures at 7 a.m. and it was the fastest shooting session I've ever had.

EARLY 20th CENTURY FEED BAGS

BERNIE BLACKSTONE'S OLD SADDLE — Thought it would be a good idea to do a portrait of a saddle which was 80 years old and unwanted.

1880'S STILL LIFE WITH FRONTIER COLT

OLD ARMY COLT, STILL LIFE, OLD TRAIL TOWN, CODY, WYOMING

This was the first painting I did of my wife. A young horse had just
broken its leg and was shot and you can sense the sadness in the dogs too.

BOB "SLIM" WARREN — an old
cowpuncher whom I waited three
years to meet. Have painted him six
times and never tire of it. He is a
classic of his type.

TOM LAIRD — A real living
prospector who also cuts firewood
for a living. He won a purple heart
in World War II and again in Korea
and thought the army surplus pack
he wears to gather stones would
be appropriate and place him in
contemporary time.

ROY BEGONA — Born in 1890
he has done everything, homesteading,
shepherding, cowboying and was a
reservoir of knowledge and an entré
to the old West.

18

WAGONS IN THE SNOW — We lived on Bob Meyer's ranch for 2½ years and every time it snowed it was magic. These wagons were very old and great subject matter.

HENRY WESTERMAN is an old time cowboy who is 82 and still rides horseback and is a wonderful old guy.

A more serious painting of my wife, Lynne, who is a photographer and environmentalist and without whose encouragement I could not have done what I have out West.

TIMBER JACK JOE, MOUNTAIN MAN, CROW AGENCY, MONTANA

19

OLD CROW
INDIAN SHELF

The Bama Method

I've been asked to describe my working procedure. Generally, this is how it goes:

I begin with a careful pencil sketch to determine the size and proportions of the anticipated finished painting. Then I do a color sketch or two, quite small. I like to find out if it will hold up without detail.

I always work on gesso panels with oils, but I doctor the surface with Shiva underpainting white to give it more texture. Then, I pencil in the drawing with a 4H or 6H and fix it thoroughly.

Next, I "key" my color scheme to the background color and lay in a semi-opaque wash over the whole panel (but transparent enough to read the pencil lines beneath). Then, I lay in the *whole* painting before finishing any one area. Usually, but not always, I do the center of interest first and then relate the rest of the painting to it. It involves softening distracting edges and lowering values to decrease their contrast. I almost always make up my own color scheme, but keep it within the realm of the original subject matter.

Mostly, I use flat sable brushes in all sizes and small rounded watercolor brushes for minute detail. When the sables lose their sharp edges I demote them for use in scumbling in preliminaries in new paintings.

As time goes on I tend to work thinner and thinner. I have come to feel that overly rich textures can become a "crutch" if used indiscriminately.

When the painting is finished, I apply a coat of temporary retouch varnish for "morale" to restore the richness of values and color which have faded due to my use of plain turpentine as a medium.

I use a butcher's tray as a palette and a curtain rod as a mahl stick. Before I begin each morning I remix my colors with a little oil to restore the desired body. I cover them every night with aluminum foil to retard drying. And for whatever it may matter I prefer to work sitting down. The editor says that with my kind of detail one should sit down to *look* at my stuff! ∎

CHESTER MEDICINE CROW — The son of a famous Crow chief at the turn of the century. He is wearing a peace medal given his father by Woodrow Wilson in 1913 and holding his father's peace pipe. He visited us twice last summer to pose and it was very exciting.

NORTH LIGHT readers were introduced to artist Ward Brackett in the Fall, 1970 issue. Since then, he's been working on a book for us. The result is a handsome volume filled with the things all artists should know.

Here, from the book, are his thoughts on one of the painter's most challenging subjects.

A

B

Ward Brackett
PAINTING A NUDE

Painting the human figure, especially the nude, is one of the hardest things to do that I can think of. There are far more problems to be dealt with than in any other kind of painting. Unless you are able to work outdoors, your first problems will be space and lighting. You will need strong, flat light on the model as well as good light on your painting.

Getting a good pose out of your model, especially an inexperienced one, can sometimes be frustratingly difficult. Anyone who has worked very much from the figure knows that frequently the best poses are "discovered" ones — when the model is taking a break or dressing or in a similarly unguarded attitude. There is something artificial and contrived looking about the "set" pose models usually get into. The model who is told to "stand with your weight on your left leg — put your hand on your hip — now look over your shoulder", can scarcely be expected to come up with anything very exciting to paint. Try to avoid the art school pose. Work for "off beat", unexpected poses. Take note of the "awkward grace" of so many of Degas' and Lautrec's dancing girls and prostitutes. Don't ignore the sensual aspect of the nude. Did you ever see a prissy nude by Gauguin, Rubens, or Modigliani? The best models, invariably, are the ones who are able to abandon themselves completely to naturalness.

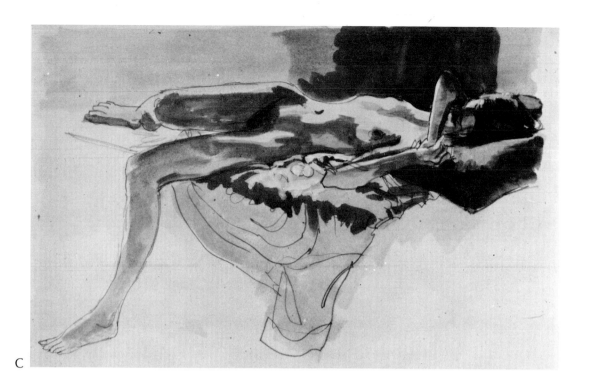

C

D

Backgrounds should be kept simple and uncontrived if you want the figure to dominate. If the figure is to become an integral part of the picture plan you must keep a relationship going between it and all the other elements of the composition. For example — the curves (or angles) of the figure can be made and should be made to contrast interestingly and dynamically with any curves or angles in the background. There should be interaction between figure and background in the form of contrasts and repeats.

Figures a, b, c, and d are drawings from my sketchbook. I'm going to take one of them, figure c, and make a painting from it. I also took a photograph of this pose to refer to in this demonstration.

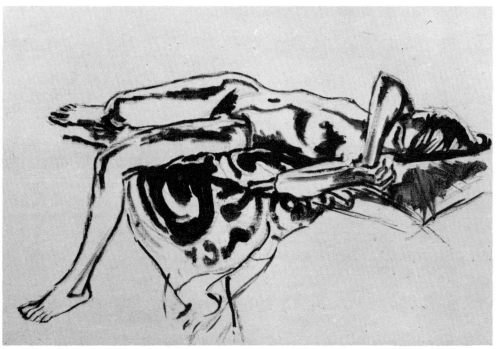

STAGE 1

When you are standing six to ten feet from a human figure, especially an undraped one, structural form had better not be taken lightly if your objective is realism. In still life, for instance, all kinds of liberties can be taken with bottles, fruit, flowers, etc. However, the closer you stand to the figure, the more critical become the problems of proportion and structural form.

Like the still life and landscape, this will be a dark-to-light sequence, but this time I tint the panel first with a light wash of raw sienna and permanent green. Now I lay in the figure and robe with burnt umber, using a #2 bristle round. I try to keep a rhythmic, flowing action to this brushwork without bothering to follow the charcoal guide-lines with complete accuracy. This stage of the painting should have plenty of dash and spirit.

2.

STAGE 2

The foundation is in. Now for the skin tone, starting with the shadow color. It would seem fairly simple to render this area in a single solid tone; but it would also be pretty un-interesting. Within this solid mass of color are many subtle variations and changes from warm to cool. In painting flesh I use the following colors: orange, cadmium red light, crimson, yellow oxide (ochre), raw sienna, burnt sienna, viridian, thalo blue, and a little, but very little white. Sometimes it's hard to decide how to apply the paint — along the forms or across them. I've found that varying the direction of the brush strokes is more interesting and in addition, seems to "knit" the painting together. How-ever, the last thing I want to suggest is that there is any rule to this.

3.

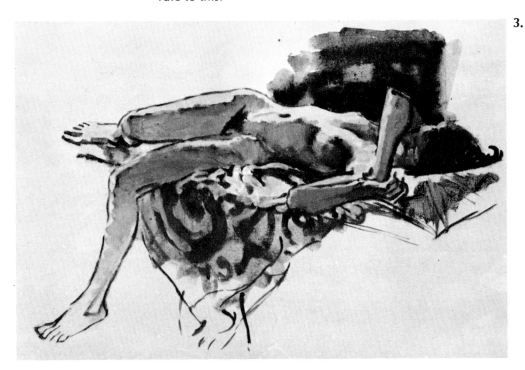

STAGE 3

Before doing anything more to the figure I indicate the robe in a soft pale green. Anything much stronger than this might make the figure appear to be floating in mid-air. This green, consisting of viridian, raw sienna, and just a touch of white, is mostly transparent — I want my under-painting to work for me. A word of warning about folds. Drapery is a fascinating subject in itself. If you allow your folds to become overworked or overcomplicated they are apt to upstage the figure. Keep them simple even if it means leaving them "unfinished"

In putting in the hair, I first reinforce the underpainting with burnt umber — then finish it off with burnt sienna, thalo blue and only enough white to lighten it slightly. It looks a litle mousey here but I can liven it up later.

NUDE STUDY by WARD BRACKETT — acrylics

STAGE 4

In the final stage I get back to the light-struck areas of the figure. These areas require crisp, clear, extremely high-key colors that are very close in value. I use cadmium yellow light, orange, cadmium red light, yellow ochre, viridian and/or thalo blue for the cooler tints. And of course, plenty of white. Now I heighten the hair color a little with warm accents of burnt sienna, raw sienna, cobalt blue, and a dab of white mixed together. Then a few notes of local color are added to the robe. A touch of color in the pillow and I call it finished before I start picking at unessential details.

Learn to recognize when any one part of your painting looks right as an element of the whole design even though it may not seem to follow your original plan for it at the time. Leave it alone and develop other elements of the painting; then come back to it. Very likely, it won't need to be changed at all.

Range of flesh colors in light areas   Flesh colors used in shadow areas

"How do you mix flesh tones?" is a question I hear about as often as any other I can think of. Aside from the obvious reasons of race and pigmentation other factors are just as important: light conditions and reflected color from surrounding areas for example. Flesh tone that appears one color in sunlight will take on an entirely different color under a cloudy gray sky. Reflected colors such as brightly colored clothing will affect skin tones considerably, especially in portraits. If I have any formula for mixing flesh color it might be the following combination, one I find myself using frequently: cadmium red light, yellow ochre, viridian green (or its equivalent, depending on the manufacturer), and white. These four colors will give a wide range of tones, from the palest blonde to rich, ruddy brunette. For cooling flesh tones there is no substitute for viridian. I'd be lost without it. ∎

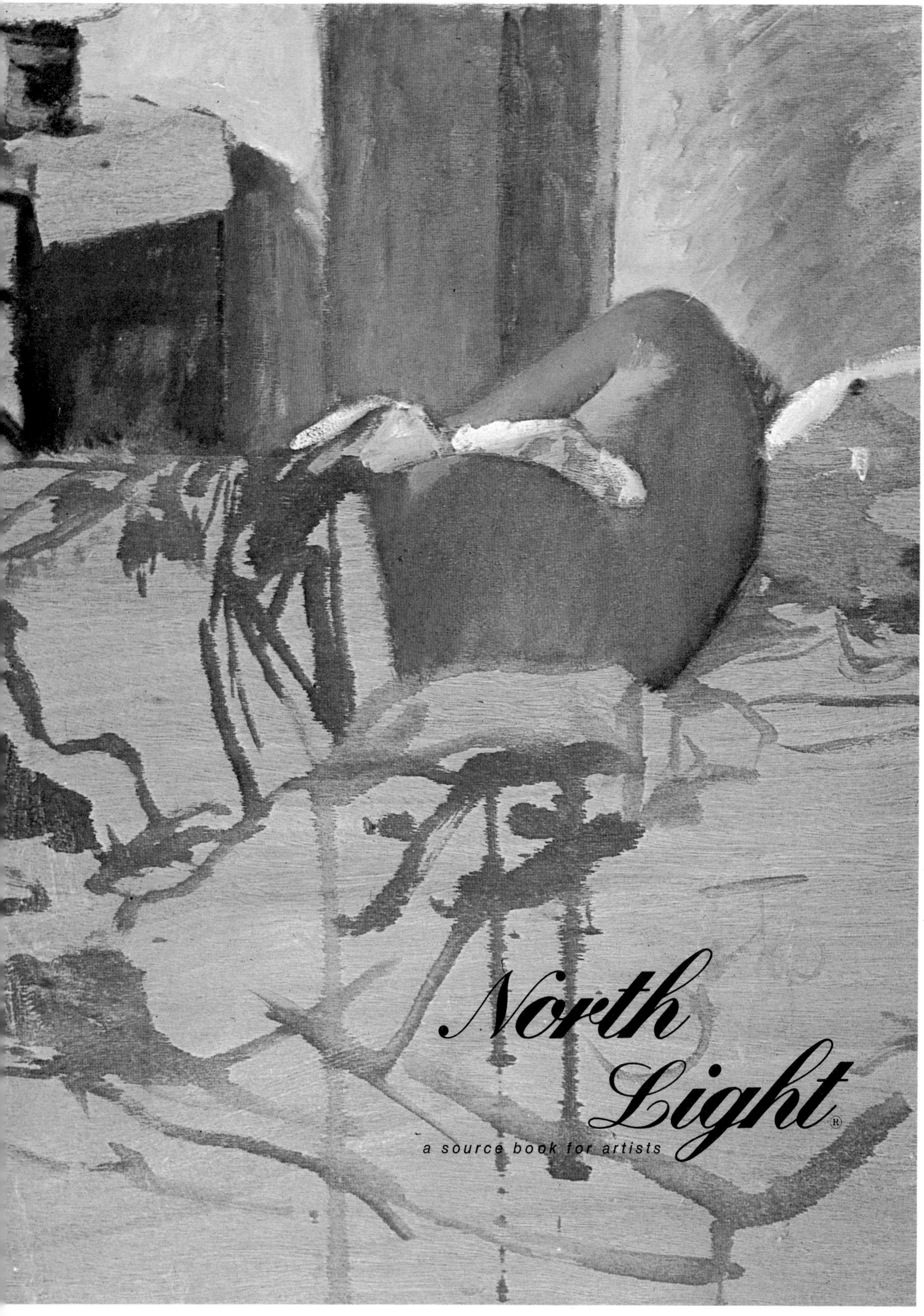
North Light®
a source book for artists

Austin Briggs in France

Austin Briggs died in Paris before this issue went to press.

He was an intimate for many years so there was a great deal of time to muse on him before it became necessary to write in the past tense.

Artists regard artist-friends on more than one level: there is the friendship and then there is the whole private world of their work and beliefs and their effect on you. In Austin's case it was a deeply rewarding thing. For one of his qualities was the ability to talk and to listen to others talk about the visual world. It was possible to reveal and explore one's aims and hopes and personal delvings with him on the most intimate terms with no fear of embarrassment for overboard effusions or dark depressions.

It was a joy to see an exhibition separately, then to discuss it with him and swap discoveries. These sessions always led to further enlightenment — often to deeper insights into a painter or sculptor — or just as rewarding; they opened one's eyes to the shallowness of a limited talent.

As I look back on many such times, I'm re-impressed by his special ability to say things that stuck and to cause his listener to reach beyond the banalities of shop talk and glib appraisals.

Articulate, intelligent people do that to you. He was both. Beyond that of course, was a walloping talent. A talent that gave him two separate careers as an illustrator — the last one an overwhelming success that he gave up because of a combination of poor health, boredom and a desire to live a whole new kind of life. This life was centered in Paris — a place he adored.

The paintings and drawings shown in this issue were among the last things he did. The picture captions are in his own words.

There were no deadlines — no manuscripts — no meddlers to keep them from being anything he wanted them to be.

He was free of those fetters. And then alas, there was suddenly no more time.

HOWARD MUNCE

This painting was done in Provence and is characteristic of that lovely part of France. The large area of violet on the right in the middle distance is a field of lavender — one of the spring crops grown for its commercial value as scent.

On the road to Cavaillon, a small town in Provence not far from the famous Provencial city of Avignon. We rent a beautiful old house in a village called Merindol each summer and usually drive on this road each morning to buy the newspaper and shop for our food supplies for the day.

29

A quick color sketch to record
the glow of the cat's eyes contrasted
with the bar of sunlight across
the patio floor.

below, Jardin de L'

PROVENCAL SKY — This, like the other paintings, was done in "mixed media" — principally a combination of gouache and oil. I usually lay in broad areas with gouache because it dries fast enough to allow many changes of mind before I settle on what I want to do.

31

"I usually do several rough sketches of the subject"   "sometimes I do a collage after the sketch"

BOUILLABAISSE

ALFRED C. CHADBOURN born Izmir, Turkey, of American parents in 1921 — studied Chouinard Art Institute, Los Angeles, Beaux-Arts and L'Academie de la Grande Chaumiere Paris.

First exhibition in 1949 Galerie Mohrien, Paris under the auspices of Jean Cocteau — 1950 Galerie Creuze, Paris.

ONE MAN SHOWS: De Cordova-Dana Museum, Lincoln, Mass., 1953, Grand Central Moderns, N.Y.C. 1954, Kipnis Gallery, Westport, Conn. 1955-57, Obelisk Gallery, Washington, D.C. 1957, Portland Museum, Maine 1959, Galerie Gregoire, Marseille 1971.

PERMANENT COLLECTIONS: Los Angeles County Museum, Chicago Art Institute, Adelphi College, N.Y., Wadsworth Atheneum, Hartford, Conn., Boston Museum of Fine Arts, National Academy, New York.

PRIVATE COLLECTIONS: Hon. Douglas Dillon, N.Y., Princess Grace of Monaco, Ambassador Arthur K. Watson, Paris, Mrs. Christian Herter, Washington, D.C., Jean Cocteau, Paris, Sir Lawrence Olivier, London.

AWARDS: Best in Landscape-Silvermine Guild, New Canaan, Conn. 1958, Louis Comfort Tiffany Fellowship 1959, Honorable Mention — Boston Festival of Arts 1957, Henry Ward Purchase Award — National Academy 1964. Elected Associate Member of National Academy, N.Y. 1970. Elected Member National Academy, N.Y. 1972.

# of palettes & palates...
the luscious still-lifes of Chip Chadbourn

During my studies at the Ecole des Beaux Arts in Paris after World War II, I enrolled as a sort of sideline in the Cordon Bleu cooking school for classes held once a week for amateurs. These were serious affairs with six of us surrounding a large working table following step by step the directions of the chef-professeur as he prepared the ingredients for the dish at hand. Seeing all the objects spread before us — fresh vegetables and herbs, meat, fowl or fish with accompanying cooking utensils, and arrays of gleaming copper pots and casseroles was always an inspiring visual experience. My career as a master chef was interrupted abruptly, however, when the Veteran's Administration caught up with me one day while I was delicately flaming a duck — "You're supposed to be an artist, not a cook" I was told. Reluctantly I hung up my white apron, although I have been cooking and painting food still lifes ever since.

Studying in Paris had many advantages. It seemed so natural to be an artist there. We were taken for granted in the everyday scheme of life which made one feel less isolated. Also, the French make great use of posters to announce their many art shows. So going to galleries became a habit like chewing gum or reading the newspapers. It's almost impossible to walk more than a block in any direction without being confronted with a colorful poster announcing a new exhibit. Rainy days in Paris were always great for museum going. I am amazed how seldom many artists I know in Westport go to galleries in New York City which is only an hour away. Whether or not one cares for contemporary trends in art, I think it's important to see what's going on — it's part of the involvement.

Now on to the business at hand . . .

In the accompanying painting my sources of inspiration were the various ingredients that go into a fish stew or Americanized version of Bouillabaisse.

I usually do several rough sketches of the subject; first going into my files for drawings I have saved over the years. Sometimes I refer to photographs if the particular material isn't at hand, but I much prefer a sketch. No matter how unfinished, it is more valuable to me, as I can remember the exact character and smell of the time and place. While I draw, I concentrate on the composition and the overall black and white pattern of the set up. For these sketches I find a Wolff carbon pencil useful as it gives me a solid, rich black. ▶

33

KITCHEN LARDER
Pennsylvania Academy 1958. These various dishes, casseroles and cooking vessels sitting on my kitchen shelves attracted me to this subject. I've always found it useful to look around my own environment for subject matter.

BOUILLABAISSE Another version of the painting p. 16 with a different arrangement. An infinite variety of ideas can be developed using the same theme.

Sometimes I do a collage after the sketch using bits of cut-out colored paper. This helps me organize the color statement into flat shapes.

Before I commit my final drawing I find it useful to first rub a light tone into the canvas. Then I block in the elements with umber and turpentine. I keep the drawing rather loose, so that mistakes can be rubbed out with a rag. With the collage or reference, I approximate the local color of the large areas — the orange pot — black stove pipe — frying pan — white dishes — blue fish — red lobsters, etc. I like to move around the entire canvas establishing color relationships from one area to another. I pay no particular attention to form at this stage.

During this period I try to keep the painting fluid and flexible. When I'm lucky and get deeply involved in the painting, several changes may take place without my awareness. If I move a large mass here and move another plane there, it would be hard for me to explain exactly why I did it. I believe a painting has certain dictates over the artist which tells him when something feels right or wrong.

No particular light source was used, as I wanted the light to exist in the painting itself. Cast shadows are used primarily as shapes rather than an explanation of a light condition. Perhaps that's what De Koonig meant when he said "Abstract shapes have a likeness too."

The final stages of the painting is a further refinement of the character development of the subject which visually inspired me at the original concept.

I was fortunate in knowing Georges Braque and visited him several times at his house in Normandie. The thing that impressed me most, I think, was his studio, which was crammed with plants and bouquets of flowers crowded against bottles and jars and tubes of paint and brushes. It was like walking into one of his still lifes. Reflecting that he had been painting these same subjects for over fifty years, I was astonished how fresh and exciting the unfinished canvases appeared. These were scattered about the room on five or six easels. For those who criticize Braque for being only a painter of still lifes he would answer "Progress in Art does not consist in extending one's limitations but in knowing them better."

FOOD This represents the cooking ingredients strewn on the kitchen table after marketing. The casual arrangement sometimes offers a better solution for a picture than a carefully planned set up.

STILL LIFE WITH BLUE PITCHER These are all familiar objects I find around my house.
If the subject is meaningful to you chances are it will make your statement clearer to the viewer.

EDITOR'S NOTE: It would be inaccurate to type Chadbourn as one who does *only* food paintings — witness the next three examples of his work.

SPANISH VILLAGE Ranger Purchase award — National Academy 1964. This landscape was
done from numerous sketches and color notes during a trip to Spain in 1949. The strong light
and dark contrasts of these sun-drenched villages offered many dramatic possibilities.

CAFE DES ST. PERES
I used to have lunch in this
cafe when I was a student
in Paris. The food was cheap
and ample and I made
sketches on the paper napkins
while Madame and her cat
watched over the customers
and cash register behind the
zinc bar. This painting was
developed from sketches done
twenty-five years ago.

**THE MILITARY
ESTABLISHMENT**
Circa 1914. The spiked
helmets and dripping medals
worn by the Kaiser and
General Von Moltke of
World War I represents to
me a culmination of all war
machines. I guess I've always
been a little frightened by
generals.

NORTH LIGHT

... a source book for artists ®

SPECIAL ISSUE

The Children's Book Field

Sept./Oct./1973

A classic drawing by John Tenniel for Alice's Adventures in Wonderland

A sad and erroneous supposition of many artists is that one of these days they'll "knock off a kid's book."

Only ignorance of this very specialized field and a misreading of the sometimes deceptively simple looking work could lead to such folly.

Easy it ain't.

Demanding and often difficult it surely is.

Because of the increasing interest in this wildly mushrooming field, NORTH LIGHT is devoting this issue to a look at the great variety of work available and in demand.

Superb artists are already established and kept constantly busy. However, new talent is continually being sought.

To give you a further professional insight into this field NORTH LIGHT has asked Carol Bancroft, Art Agent for Publishers Graphics in Westport, Conn. to give the uninitiated some tips from her every day experience, and to seek comment from some of the leading art directors, buyers and editors in the Children's book field.

Ms. Bancroft's background includes staff work for Ladies Home Journal, McCall's and Woman's Day. She has also been Art Director, Junior Books, for McGraw Hill.

Publishers Graphics whom she now represents is part of a phenomena new to the publishing field. In addition to the more than 50 free lance artists they represent, they maintain an independent, fully-staffed and equipped studio employing 20 artists who design formats, deal in type, photography, mechanical assembly — total production.

They ready this entire package for publishers, thereby relieving them of the need for large standby staffs. Publishers Graphics is headed by Verne Bowman and Miller Pope. In New York City Mulvey-Crump Assocs. Inc., Craven & Evans, and Design Council of New York perform similar services.

NORTH LIGHT readers in other sections of the country can find other such groups listed in the all-inclusive book, *Literary Market Place,* which most public libraries carry.

It's an exciting field, generally sparse in pay but creatively challenging and satisfying.

The Art of Art for Kids

The children's book field is generally divided into two groups: *Educational* and *Trade* (juvenile). Educational books are distributed to schools. Trade books go to libraries and book stores.

TRADE, THE JUVENILE JUNKET

Although juvenile (or junior books) are also marketed to book stores, they are mainly marketed to public and school libraries. Their readership level is pre-school through high school.

Picture books, heavy on illustrations (4-6 age level) are often author-illustrated. Editors seem to prefer this. But there are exceptions when a creative illustrator can grasp the real meaning of a story and illuminate its text.

A lot of art is also used in books of the 8-12 age level. The subjects are as vast and varied as they are fun. They are both fiction and non-fiction and run from fantasy, folk and fairy tales, to science, adventure, math, history, art and sports.

These two areas, picture books and books for the middle years, give the artist the best exposure, and open educational doors as well.

Teen novels usually carry less inside illustration, but their jackets need sparkling poster-like graphics to help sell them.

Good juvenile book illustration should be so alive and imaginative that it is worthy of adult fascination.

More than ever, Editors are open to new talent. They seek artists with the ability to draw, (a rarer quality than you might suppose) who are innovative and creative, who have the ability to *design* and do lay-out plus a working knowledge of production.

I am constantly being asked if a particular artist knows about color separation (working with overlays.)
(See Studio Rap Section on page 21)

Most juvenile (trade) books today are printed in black, black plus one color, or black plus two colors (three colors). Editors tell me that only about three books out of their thirty will be printed in full color this year.

Most assignments begin with pencil idea sketches from the manuscript. When these are approved, you are considered a kind of co-author. That is, you, in some cases, choose the colors and type face. You pace the pages, position the type along with your art and seek a format that flows from page to page with interest and variety.

Evenness of style and technique throughout is another quality to strive for.

Trade books pay either a "flat fee" or on an advance-royalty basis. On flat fee, they pay just one set amount, usually one-half on signing of the contract and one-half on completion of the job.

Royalty is more complicated, but with a good author-publisher combination, it can be very lucrative.

If a moderate number of illustrations are used, the illustrator is often paid just a flat fee. However, a highly pictured book is usually paid in royalties. Here the author and the artist split the royalties. Each gets 5% of the list price. They each first receive an "advance" against the royalty. No royalties are paid to the artist and author until what adds up to the advance figures in sales is paid back to the publisher. So it takes about a year or two till the royalty checks come in. If a royalty book is printed in paperback form and uses the same illustrations, the artists gets an additional fee. Also, if the book is printed abroad (foreign rights) the artist gets more money.

THE TEXTBOOK TALE (Educational books)

The "Dick and Jane" books of a short while back have changed. Now, these educational books are picture-packed to show and tell.

Textbooks are only a part of today's teaching tools. Activity cards, posters, games, spellers, film strips, magazines and encyclopedias are some of the many media for lesson learning.

Students' ages range from kindergarten through twelfth grade and subjects range from science, social studies, history and language to art, literature and math.

In educational publishing, most art buying is done by designers/art editors. The larger houses have team leaders to contact.

What do educational art buyers buy? Anything from a four color realistic Civil War battle scene to a black and white sketch of a sitting sea gull. These buyers need a little of everything.

The mixed ethnic scene — blacks, Puerto Ricans, Spanish-Americans, Mexican-Americans, Chinese, Japanese, Indians are very much "in" these days. Kids as individuals are all-important to this field. Cuteness alone will get you nowhere. You must know what kids are all about — what they think, what they wear — what they're into today. Superficiality is out; truth is in.

Basically, the movement is toward trade book art. Educational art buyers are influenced by the best sellers in the juvenile market. Ray Cruz and Ron Himler are as popular in the school scene as they are with public libraries and book stores.

Educational art buyers are concerned with visual competition in all media. Fresh, new, innovative, lively, experimental, sophisticated, entertaining — are their cries. Nothing should limit the imagination of the young reader.

cont. P.45

Varieties of Realism

George Sottung

David Brown

Kees DeKiefte

Jack Hearne

Uldis Klavins

Al Michini

Kees DeKiefte

Al Muenchen

Edward Vebell

Illustration by Jack Hearne, Reprinted from
THE NEW BOOK OF KNOWLEDGE, by permission of
the publishers, Grolier Incorporated.

Illustration by Ward Brackett.
Reproduced from *WIDENING CIRCLES* by Margaret Early et al.
Copyright © 1970 by Harcourt Brace Jovanovich, Inc. by
permission of the illustrator and publisher.

Humor in many manners

Marylin Hafner

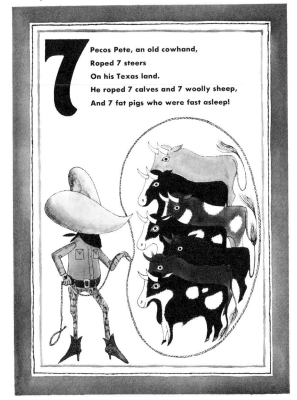

7

Pecos Pete, an old cowhand,
Roped 7 steers
On his Texas land.
He roped 7 calves and 7 woolly sheep,
And 7 fat pigs who were fast asleep!

Gahan Wilson

Paul Harvey

A. O. Williams

Paul Harvey

What Art Buyers in the Juvenile field want.

TED SCHROEDER — *A. D., Garrard Publishing, Scarsdale, N.Y.*
I look for, but find very little good humor and design. Most artists are too style conscious and don't have a real feeling for children.

MARGARET FRITH — *Exec. Ed., Coward-McCann, N.Y.C.*
Publishers are always looking for new illustrators. Books are a fine way to reach a large audience. A single painting is a one time thing and available to only a few. A book offers a means to reach many. Portfolios should go beyond the projects you did in art school. Animals and people and the interpretation of a favorite story give the publisher a good idea about the artist's potential.

JAMES MURPHY — *Asst. to the Editor, Seaberry Press, N.Y.C.*
The artist should know the difference between picture books and the "8 to 12" age areas. He should show samples aimed at either group. Knowledge of book pacing as well as production is essential. Interesting faces and characterizations are as important.

KATHERINE ERNST — *Asst. V.P. and Senior Ed., Prentice Hall, Englewood Cliffs, N.J.*
I look for good, believable alive figures and specific kids with character. I also look for clean, visually pleasing graphics and layouts along with convincing mood and tone.

GRACE CLARK — *A. D., Random House, N.Y.C.*
Many artists give little thought to how children look at things; there is a special kind of feeling involved.

BARBARA LUCAS — *Ed.-in-Chief, G. P. Putnam's Sons, N.Y.C.*
I like to see finished art work along with sketches. I suggest an artist choose a story already done (even an original manuscript) and illustrate it. I like to see what the artist has chosen to illustrate . . . his rhythm and pacing throughout a few pages. Artist should also submit samples to show he knows how to do color separation.

WILMA GOTTLIEB — *A. D., Henry Z. Walck Inc., N.Y.C.*
Illustrators who want to do children's books should show appropriate art and not art designed for magazine and advertising. I like to see how the artist would pace a book — to see flow of action from page to page. The artist should also be capable of doing jacket art.

RIKI LEVINSON — *A. D., E. P. Dutton and Co., N.Y.C.*
I look for an individual quality, warmth — ability to draw well (not just technique that tries to cover an inability to draw) — sincere approach to the story being illustrated — a close relationship visually to the story. Too often artists illustrate in a vacuum which tells nothing about their thinking capacity. I suggest that new illustrators take an existing text of a book and make a rough dummy with two or three finished illustrations to show how they would handle a book.

ALAN BENJAMIN — *A. D., Charles Scribners and Sons, N.Y.C.*
The artist should show a character in more than one situation (ability to follow story). Several styles should be presented as well as an ability to do pre-separated colors.

cont. P. 15

According to the recent Children's Book Section in the New York Times, learners retain about 10% of what they read, 20% of what they hear, and 30% of what they see.

Here's how an assignment in the Educational field usually works:
unlike Trade, in most cases art "specs" are given. These are instructions as to exact size, shape, color, plus description as to what needs to be illustrated. "Girl age 8 in pink dress, polishing floor near a white poodle who sits on a silver sink like a stuffed toy."

Production understanding again is a must. Knowing color separation, sizing, scaling, etc., is vital. Check your nearest art schools, school extension programs and special interest groups for production courses.

You will undoubtedly put a lot of hours in your first job and make only a little money, but you'll get a good sample in return . . . and hopefully more work.

THE CARE AND FEEDING OF YOUR PORTFOLIO

How you have your work matted and mounted says a lot about you when you show samples. Present your work and yourself as professionally as possible at all times. Your portfolio should be a size you can carry conveniently. One gal, just out of art school, couldn't get in my door. Her work was in large cartons! Slides (35 mm transparencies) would have made a compact portfolio. Most art buyers have a light box, or you can

A. O. Williams

buy an inexpensive portable electric viewer. An invaluable aid in showing your work is L M P, "Literary Market Place", published by R. R. Bowker Co. This is an annual, soft-cover directory listing the names and titles of the principal staff members of all the national publishers. Your local library probably has it. If you can afford a printed mailer, it makes a good reminder of you and your work. If you don't live anywhere near the principal publishing cities, it's less costly than shipping heavy samples back and forth.

Persistent promotion plays a large part in getting work. Every six months, at least, you should send out new promotional samples for art buyers to keep.

The Society of Illustrators' (128 East 63rd Street, New York, N.Y.) annual show has an unpublished category. If your work is accepted and hung in their show, it automatically gets published in the Illustrators Annual. Your name appears under your illustration, with your address listed in the back of the book. This book is the Bible of most art buyers.

Having an agent is a very good way to get your things around to publishers without having to go yourself. You save on shoe leather, energy and most of all, time, especially when some educational publishing houses have as many as forty different art editors. The best way to find a good agent is to ask art buyers who deal with them constantly.

C.B.

Decorative styles

Lynn Sweat

Alfred Olschewski

Naiad Einsel

47

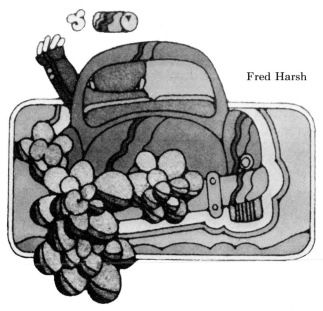

Fred Harsh

John Cavallo

Susan Anderson

ANN BENEDUCE — *V.P., Ed.-in-Chief, Thomas Crowell, N.Y.C.*
An artist should be able to do all kinds of artwork from the most literal to the most abstract, from conservative to far out, plus have solid draftsmanship. A mastering of technique within the medium an artist chooses to use is essential. The artist should be able to interpret a manuscript with sensitivity and without being restricted by his own limitations. I look for a strong design sense plus individual and interesting style. Evidence of wit and creative intelligence are signs that the artist will not only be able to understand and interpret an author's manuscript, but that he can add an extra dimension of his own.

Educational Art Buyers tell what they are looking for in a portfolio.

ANNIKA UMANS — *Art Ed., Houghton-Mifflin, Boston.*
An artist must first of all recognize his limitations; also I'd like to be sure an artist can follow a story line and/or a character through a story. Any artist who is really keen to do children's illustrations, should keep on doing life drawings. I want to see an artist draw one child in all the different movements that the story requires: running, kneeling, etc.; and that he can master all the facial expressions — crying, anger, etc.

MORT PERRY — *A. D., McGraw-Hill (Webster Division) N.Y.C.*
Portfolios should be compact and precise as possible; should not be repetitious. Use discrimination in what is shown.

WHIT VYE — *Illustration Dir., Xerox Education Publications, Middletown, Ct.*
Most important is basic drawing skills. Then be experimental and innovative.

GEORGE McCLAIN — *A. D., Allyn & Bacon, Boston*
Originality, professionalism and a good presentation show how an artist works and feels about his art. Through the use of a variety of media you can learn of his versatility.

FRANK LUCAS — *A. D., Ginn and Company, Lexington, Mass.*
When an artist stops experimenting, he is dead. Stiff drawings have been out since 1968. We're communicating to kids who want to interpret and who, today, are sophisticated. Also important is a clean presentation and a knowledge of production. Knowing sizing, scaling, and pre-separation is just as important as the art.

GINNY COPELAND — *A. D., McGraw-Hill, Webster Division, Kansas City, Mo.*
I look for what an illustrator "enjoys doing best". Colorful, humanistic and whimsical art, along with solid production.

ARTHUR SOARES — *A. D., Prentice Hall, Englewood Cliffs, N.J.*
Style is important. An illustrator should have obviously clear control over the medium he uses, coupled with problem solving ability and a true understanding of the subject.

KATHY REYNOLDS — *Art Ed., Houghton-Mifflin, Boston*
I want to see experimentation, different styles. There should be only about 5-6 good samples in a portfolio. Deadline discipline and production knowledge are *very* important.

Techniques of all kinds

William Carroll

Joan Halpern

Joan Halpern

Monroe Eisenberg

Ronald Himler

A variety of line

Florian Erber

Bert Dodson

Ron Carreiro

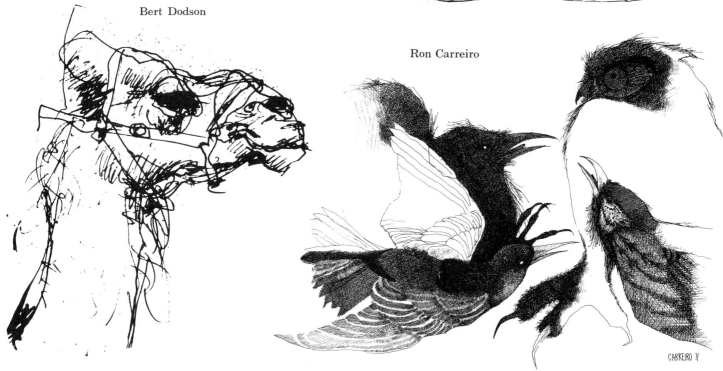

Walter Einsel
carved wood

Blake Hampton
colored paper

Three dimensional constructions

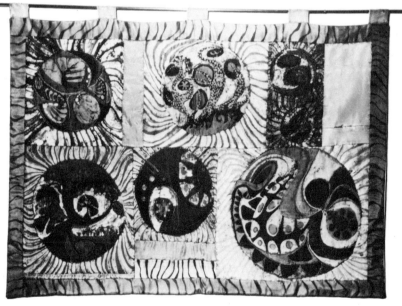

Susan Anderson—batik

Susan Swan
sewed cloth, stuffed
This puppet is one of a
series done for Random
House *Mathematics Program:
Level K.*

Dianne MacDermott—bread dough

Two typical layouts and the finished versions

Ben F. Stahl

Tom stands on a chair
and asks his mother to hold one end of the string
at the Tom mark.
Then he stretches it on up the wall
and makes another mark at the top.
"Look," he says, "this mark is two toms high.
Dad is nearly two toms tall."
Tom has measured his dad
using m special unit of measure —
his kind of unit is one tom.

He starts measuring the toms of everything —
people and walls and sidewalks.

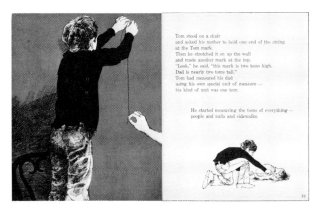

Notice the refinements in the finished
version of the spread above:
The close up of the boy; the top of the chair
tells you as much as the whole chair.
The woman's hand is all that is needed
to tell of her presence. The result is a tighter
more dramatic picture. And the squatted
cat is paying more attention than the one
strolling by in the rough.

■

Publishers
COWARD. McCANN
& GEOGHEGAN

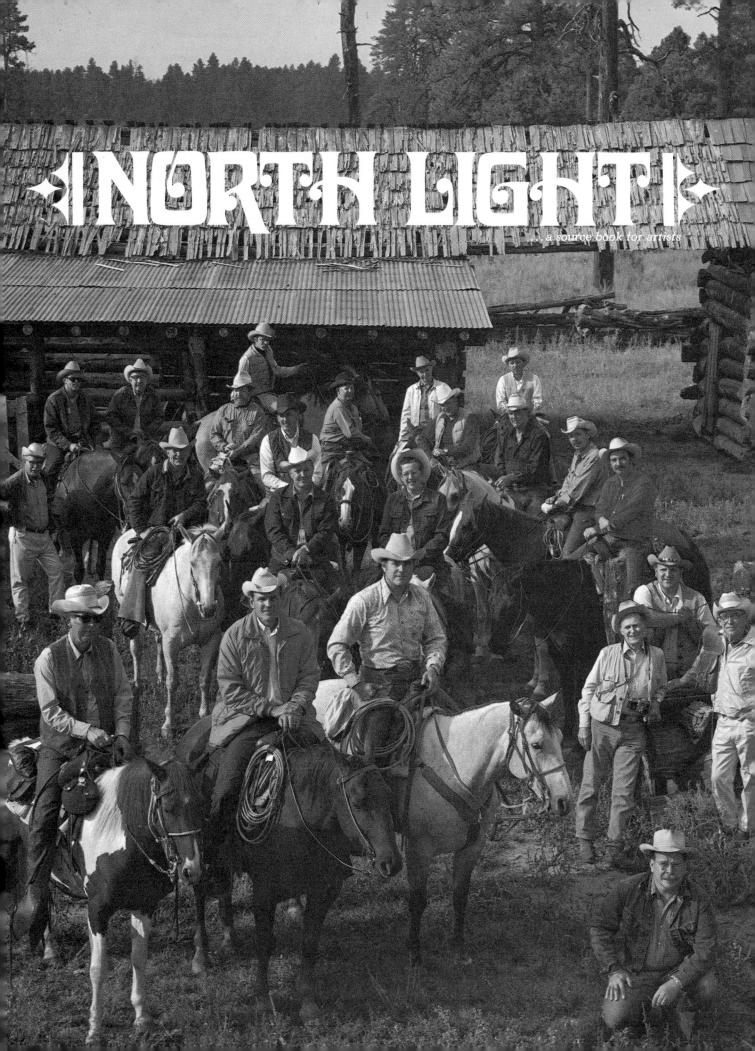

NORTH LIGHT

...a source book for artists

Presenting the work of the

Cowboy Artists

This edition of NORTH LIGHT is devoted entirely to the work of a unique band of artist-historians: the Cowboy Artists of America.

Our Walt Reed has been closely associated with them for the past few years—as a guest speaker and judge for their latest annual show and through his association with

# of America

Harold Von Schmidt on their recent collaboration: "Harold Von Schmidt Draws and Paints the Old West".

We thank U. Grant Speed, President of the Cowboy Artists and Paul Weaver of Northland Press for their cooperation in supplying us with the material herein.

H.M.

If you would ask an old-time cowboy to choose between a painting by Frederic Remington and Charles Russell, he would probably admire Remington's horses but pick the Russell. When pushed for a reason, he'd likely say that Russell was the more "savvy" in his details about cowherding.

His point would be well taken. Russell was a wrangler for several years before he became an artist — the subject was a natural part of him. Remington came West with a trained artist's eye and while he faithfully painted what he saw, he could not make the same selective judgments in stressing key details.

This is not to denigrate Remington as an artist — his horses, his troopers, his cowboys and Indians, all have their own quality of drama and history that make them important and in fact, neither artist was infallible. However, it is this vital necessity for the artist to know his subject that was a key factor in the formation of the Cowboy Artists.

It began casually enough. Joe Beeler, Charlie Dye and John Hampton had gone down to visit a roundup near Magdelina, Mexico, back in November 1964. It was an old fashioned festival of riding, roping and cowboying by top hands. On the way back, discussing the highlights, and artist friends who had missed seeing it, the idea of forming an association with other area artists to preserve this western heritage got started.

Response was quick and enthusiastic. An organization meeting was held in Sedona, Arizona. By-laws which relied heavily on the local County Sheriff's Posse by-laws were drawn up. Included was a clause stating, "The purpose and the objective of the Cowboy Artists of America is to record, preserve and perpetuate the culture of the American West as it was and is now and to insure the authentic representation of that way of life during all of its historical and contemporary existence."

The John Clymer painting on the preceding spread won the Gold Medal for Oil Painting. It's titled **"Moving Camp"**.

First Prize: **WATERCOLOR**
DONALD TEAGUE: Gold Medal winner

WAITING FOR TROUBLE. Watercolor, 20″ x 30″.

THE PRICE OF A HERD. Bronze, 10" high.

 First Prize: **SCULPTURE.**
WILLIAM MOYERS: Gold Medal winner.

Plans to hold an important first exhibition got a big boost when Dean Krakel, Director of the National Cowboy Hall of Fame and Western Heritage Center in Oklahoma City, offered those facilities and the showing was held in September, 1966.

From the beginning, the exhibitions have been a financial and artistic success. With most of the originals of Russell, Remington, Schreyvogel, Farny and other early Western painters already tied up in museum collections, private collectors were eager to find contemporary works of comparable quality.

The Cowboy Hall presented medals and made prize awards for the best works in several categories. First prize winners became purchase awards for the Hall Collection. Each year has seen additional gains. Recently in conjunction with the show two day seminars on various aspects of Western Art, historic and contemporary, have been held, with experts in history, art and western research as guest speakers.

Most Cowboy Artists members are serious researchers and avid collectors of western artifacts themselves, with studios resembling museums filled with everything from guns, beads, arrowheads and moccasins to saddles and buffalo hides. And, to keep active, many members put regular time in the saddle.

An integral part of the Cowboy Artists program is the Trail Ride, held in a different part of the West each year.

JOE BEELER
DENEH (The People) : Bronze, 26″ high.

ROBERT LOUGHEED: Gold Medal winner.
First Prize: **MIXED MEDIA.**
WEARING THE BELL BRAND. Acrylic, 12″ x 24″.

Although the annual shows have not been juried, the exhibiting membership is restricted to the best professionals and qualifications for new members are high. Judges for awards have been selected from among experts in art and the old West with stress in judging placed on accuracy as well as artistry.

Anachronisms are taboo. If an artist includes a Henry rifle it had better be right, and any elements of clothing worn by cowboy, trooper or Indian must be not only authentic in detail, but also in proper date with each other.

So much of our information about the Old West has been distorted by novels or motion pictures slanted for reasons of drama or even by the "serious" reporting of the period which reflected the prevailing ethnic prejudices. The Cowboy Artists would like to set this record straight — to depict the West as it was, and is.

Has this stress on authenticity inhibited artistic creativity? Members do not believe so. The subject is still as wide open as the country itself.

It is good to know that the standards of George Catlin, Remington, Russell, Harold Von Schmidt and others are being carried on with their same dedication.

Shown here are prize winning pictures and some additional outstanding drawings and paintings from the Seventh Annual exhibit held at the Cowboy Hall.

W.R.

NICK EGGENHOFER
SIX HORSE STAGE. Watercolor, 15″ x 30″.

MELVIN WARREN: Silver Medal winner.
Second Prize: **MIXED MEDIA.**
OLD MAN OF TALPA. Pastel, 21″ x 31″.

COWBOY CAUCUS. 30″ x 52″.

 JAMES BOREN: Silver Medal winner. Second Prize: **WATERCOLOR.**

BROWNELL McGREW: Gold Medal winner. First Prize: **DRAWING.**
HOSTI 'IN CHISCHILLIE. Charcoal, 19″ x 24″.

 JIM REYNOLDS: Silver Medal winner. Second Prize: **OIL PAINTING.**

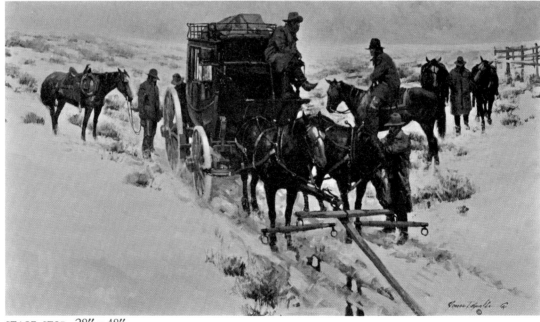

STAGE STOP. 28″ x 48″.

60

NED JACOBS: Silver Medal co-winner.
Second Prize: **DRAWING.**
PEYOTE MAN. Charcoal, 23″ x 15″.

GORDON SNIDOW: Silver Medal co-winner.
Second Prize: **DRAWING.**
HARD TIMES. Charcoal 24″ x 27″.

HARRY JACKSON
EXPRESS RIDER, bust. Bronze, 10″ high.

GRANT SPEED
STAMPEDIN' OVER A CUTBANK. Bronze, 22" high.

FRED FELLOWS WHEN COLD WINDS WARM THE HEART. Oil, 30" x 48".

ROBERT SCRIVER: Silver Medal winner.
Second Prize: SCULPTURE.
NOT FOR GLORY. Bronze, 30" high.

FRANK POLK
TIME TO SADDLE-UP. Bronze, 11" high.

TOM RYAN SOAKIN' UP. Charcoal, 12¼" x 17¼".

HARVEY W. JOHNSON WHEN MEAT TURNS BAD. Oil, 24" x 36".

The Creed and Craft of Leonard Everett Fisher

If Leonard Fisher ever had periods of doubt about purpose or direction, he doesn't have them now. His aims and beliefs are strong and uncluttered — they are presented herewith.

Fisher's father was a marine designer so his respect for precision started with that gentleman. Crooked ships are not allowed.

Later came formal art schools, World War II and Yale Art School. There, he received the Winchester Fellowship and the Pulitzer Painting Prize.

Next came Europe. Then a stint as Dean of the Whitney Art School in New Haven.

Meantime, he has illustrated 200 books and written 25.

His paintings are part of the collection of the following: Butler Institute of American Art; the Library of Congress; the New Britain Museum of American Art; the Housatonic College Museum; the Scott-Fanton Museum, the Universities of Oregon, Minnesota, Southern Mississippi; the New Haven Paint and Clay Club; the Free Library of Philadelphia.

Whoever is set to undermine the execution of art is set to destroy art — WILLIAM BLAKE

Recently, the New Britain Museum of American Art presented a twenty-four year retrospective exhibition of my art. It was one of those rare opportunities for an artist to see a good chunk of his life in one broad sweep. But it was an unsettling experience for me to see so much of the past become the present. Too many memories, too many events came between me and my objectivity.

I know what has shaped my artistic existence from my birth to the present moment. I know the route over which I have traveled — every twist, every turn. I know each watering place along the way, each bend in the road and every force that made my hands do what they did and are doing.

I like to think that I know where I am going. This inexhorable voyage, for me, is a deeply rooted compulsion founded on the premise that the projection of one's art, one's spirit, is wholly dependent upon one's execution — one's ability to manipulate his tools in the service of his intellect. The heart and soul of all this, the unmanipulative core, is an essence of all art — *humanization*. Humanization — that effort to move people toward selflessness, compassion, reason, grace and civility — is, perhaps, a futile process. Yet, however impossible, it is a compelling enough intent that should be sufficient justification for artistic creation in any mode.

I feel no guilt for being alive, nor am I so bored with the continuing miracle of life with all its empty-headed follies that I am overwhelmed by some messianic urge to assault and rearrange the senses of others at the expense of my own honest visions and humanization. What I paint, how I come to it, and why, has little to do with fashionable appearances or contrived culture. I am, willy-nilly, a child of the twentieth century.

That an artist is affected by the tapestry of events and morality that mark his time ought not to be in doubt. We are shaped by these forces in every conscious and subconscious way. My response, however, is directed toward immortal Man, the space he occupies, the space he moves in. In a sense, this is an optimistic outlook. It assumes that Man, the species, is an eternal constancy. Thus, I see painting as a memorable experience to be savored as a formidable presence in which the whole stuff of life ought to throb — a lingering experience to be contemplated as a work of art rather than as an instant and disposable design entertainment.

Now, none of what I am saying means that I am content with things as they are or seem to be. I am not interested in being a mirror; in painting duplications of tired old barns, crashing surfs, marshes at sunset, marinas at dawn, overdone still lifes, warmed over studio nudes, etc., etc. My drawing and painting spring full blown out of my head without props, set-ups, color slides and slavish references. It is aimed at that which can only be plausible within the painted

environment I provide. Essentially, I am more concerned with expressing the nature of Man's intellect than in depicting the look of him and his world. And this I try to do with familiar forms and shapes in numerous ways. It is an inverted realism whereby mind dominates matter rather than the other way around. It is chiefly perceptual rather than visual. One kind of reality (i.e. outward) is being exchanged for another kind of reality (i.e. inward).

Representational painters whose major concern is either the absolute re-creation or personal interpretation of natural appearances see me as being something less than a "faithful renderer". For some I am not "loose" and thus "expressive" enough. For others, I disobey too many rules necessary for painting things "familiarly natural". Post World War II abstractionists — my generation — on the other hand, think I am either a conservative or a surrealist since I completely render identifiable forms as seen under a light.

There are those who call me an illustrator (as a painter, not in terms of the two hundred or so books I have illustrated) because my forms and shapes *are* identifiable and seemingly story-telling from time to time. But illustrators think I am a designer and designers themselves are unmoved. Whatever relationship all this elusiveness has to the mercurial contemporary scene is beyond me. I have never given too much thought to labels, categories, visual specialties, applied philosophies and schemes of painted upmanship.

With all this in mind, and from my beginnings, I have reached for sharp focus (not hard edge) and the absolute resolution of form and space to lessen the gulf between me, my art and my audience. This sharpness, along with the scale of my pictorial matter, has increased with the passing years as has the intensity of my color. Part of this is due to my drive for more precise statements; to be better understood, as it were. Some of this is due to years of accumulated manual skill which is now habit; which I do not find burdensome; which I cannot be without; which I relish and hone toward the perfection I seek. Also, some of this is due to the character of the media I use toward these ends.

I have little patience with those who would dismiss craftsmanship, "loose" or "tight", as a technical exercise or impasse, stopping at the surface and having no connection whatever with creativity. "He is a technician", they often say; or "he's too facile", implying that manual virtuosity kills "feeling", that is to say "art". Rubbish! Craftsmanship does not automatically insure the birth of a true work of art. But it does not automatically kill it either!

Technical mastery, the combined acquired skill of hand and knowledge, is the grammar of the language of vision. It is the instrument of clear articulation, of communication — the controlled execution required to perform visually within the frame of reference. At least, is an integral part of my ultimate expression.

This is one of a few large monochromatic pieces that have little to do with preliminaries. Using a good size bristle bru[s] and black paint, I sketched in a figure design as fast as it loom[e] in my head. Next, a translucent brownish middletone was appl[ ] over the entire design excludin[ ] the white background. Using 2 values of umber for the ¾ darks, 2 or 3 values of yellow f[ ] the lights and allowing the middletone to work in betwee[n] I began to bring out the form. Lastly, a highlight here, a dark accent there, a clean up of the white background and the piec[e] is finished.

SHADOW OF A RIBBON *acrylic on gessoed masonite 48" x 48" 1970 collection: The New Britain Museum, Connecticut*

It is not the box or ribbon that has been painted here but rather the space these things have formed and contain. Sharply painted illusions such as this (i.e. where a 3 dimensional formed space is created on a spaceless plane) are greatly dependent upon the use of linear perspective, the absolute control of hues, values and intensities, the relationship between cool and warm color, and the juxtaposition of counterpoint. In this instance a spatial presence would have been noticed without the ribbon. By adding a hot, bright high-keyed ribbon having a different linear symmetry than the box, the space becomes a confirmed reality.

PAGEANT MASQUERADE *egg tempera on gessoed masonite 48" x 24" 1954 collection: J. Leonard Scheer, New York*

"Pageant" is typical of a number of early paintings that fall into the "man in fantasy" category. In this as in other egg tempera paintings, only the yolk of the egg and water is used as the painting vehicle. Whatever the color of the yolk — from rich yellow to pale yellow — it has absolutely no affect upon the water ground pigment with which it is mixed. The brushes used on such a panel as this range from #00 to 5 — all short-handled pointed sables.

AMERICAN LAMENT *gelatine size on laminated rag paper 60" x 40" 1964 collection: The Butler Art Institute, Ohio*

Full of pointed symbolism, "Lament" was painted 2 or 3 months following the assassination of John F. Kennedy. It was produced during the period I was engrossed with "man in transience". What I tried to do here was to visually articulate an immense and unspeakable tragedy rather than depict the violence of the deed.

There is no hesitation — no fumbling — between what I choose to paint and the act of painting whatever it is. This, of course, was not always so. I worked endlessly, from small boy to manhood to achieve the skill I am talking about. It did not just appear one day. In any event, I work with speed — tensely, but comfortably. Rarely do I lay in the color and values in an overall way, ponder, adjust, and then bring the work to life here, there and everywhere all at once. My pondering and planning take place long before application. Once I commit myself, however, there is no turning back. Working either background through middleground to foreground, left to right or in some specific manner determined by various factors, I finish as I go along or as much as the arrangement of the painting's parts will allow. I put it down and there it is.

While this discipline grows out of personal need, the media I choose to use requires such discipline for execution. The look of my paintings is conditioned by my needs and the nature of the media all working together, inseparably. The media themselves — egg tempera (1947-1960); gelatine size (1960-1965); acrylic (1965-   ) — are related. They are water-based; visually cool and physically thin; high keyed; and without an impression of weight and atmosphere as compared to oil paint. They dry almost upon application. This allows for instant rendering of complex forms. As I said, there is no turning back, no wiping out, only forthright commitment.

Obviously, I am not a painter who applies one medium to every changing concept that crosses his mind. I went from egg tempera to size to acrylic (and several other techniques in between) as I changed and as concepts required specific alterations in approach.

The airless, weightless, other world look of egg tempera — a look partly arrived at by stroking on the paint rather than by brushing it on with wide massive gradations (after all, things seen in "real life" are not crosshatched) — was especially suited to my ideas about "man in fantasy", a concept that occupied much of my attention during the early years. When I turned toward "man in transience", egg tempera did not seem practical at the scale I was beginning to enlarge. Instead, I experimented for a short time with an ancient drawing discipline that required a monochromatic flat middletone ground applied with glue size

(i.e. gelatine) over which was brushed a black and white "form drawing". The middletone ground acted as an intermediate value while its hue gave it a decorative flavor. A popular example of this type of linear "form description" would be Albrecht Durer's PRAYING HANDS. Adapting the technique, I produced with some difficulty large flat *poly*chromatic grounds on paper over which I linearly rendered figures in black and white. These highly modelled forms were seemingly solid and transparent at the same time. The look of these works were unique and suited my purposes. However, they became a bridge that led me to acrylic as my point of view changed. And with this change came an end to some fifteen years of painting linearly — that is to say of achieving forms, shapes, planes, etc. with short, fine strokes of color rather than with wide masses.

With acrylic I could now quickly produce larger surfaces. Also, I could rapidly complete clear, large scale monochromatic solids in three values. Moreover, I could achieve varying, almost measurable illusionary spaces with high intensity color. Passing from egg tempera through size to acrylic was a natural evolution for me rather than a wrenching shift of stylistic gears. As such, I moved from fantasy and symbolic realism to a more dimensional realism; from form in space to color in formed space. Rarely, during these transitions, did I ever allow appearance to supersede content, regardless of what new contemporary styles were swirling about me.

During the early years, fantasy, to me, spelled originality since it was wholly imaginative and inventive. Accordingly, I painted the solid, rythmical presence of my imagination. As maturity overtook me, I saw every living thing as a passing form. Only renewable life was the ever-present, constant force. Finally, I painted no living thing at all, only colorful emptiness. I suppose I was beginning to come to terms with my own mortality and those dear to me.

But life does renew. The figure is reappearing. The transition continues. Yet, whatever the quality of my powers, every creative passage I take will be underscored by an inherent sense of pride in craftsmanship. In that alone — in craftsmanship — rests much of the strength and faith in the one visible extension of human spirit — art.

WOMAN WITH A MASK
acrylic on gessoed masonite 32" x 48" 1972 collection:
J. Leonard Scheer, New York

On the opposite page are 4 basic stages in the development
of this painting. The first stage shows a charcoal drawing
defined in some areas with black paint. Only those
values from middletone downward are rendered. This is,
in a sense, an underpainting similar to the india ink
underpainting used for egg tempera. The purpose of this
is to hold the dark values of color by minimizing from the
beginning the effects of light being speedily refracted
by a brilliant white gesso ground wherever translucent
middletones and transparent darks are to be painted.
The use of such an underpinning in non-spontaneous
or non-alla prima painting helps to produce an extreme
dimensional quality. The second stage shows a translucent
green tone applied to the entire figure only. This will
have a direct affect on the final "fleshy" appearance of
the nude. Here too the background can be seen partially
finished. The third stage shows the finished background
while the fourth stage indicates the nearly completed nude.
The color reproduction is of the completed painting.

A scratchboard illustration from
THE DEATH OF EVENING
STAR, a novelette for young
adults published by Doubleday
& Co., which I also wrote.
It was executed with needle and
knife on inked-in white British
scraperboard. One of 42 illustrations created for this book, it
is typical of several thousand such
"soft engravings" I have created
for juvenile books. The American
Library Association chose this
as a "NOTABLE CHILDREN'S
BOOK FOR 1972".

71

INVITATION TO IMMORTALITY *egg tempera on gessoed masonite 48" x 36" 1951 collection: Joseph M. Erdelac, Ohio*

Another "man in fantasy" piece. This painting reaches more openly for symbolism than others of the same vintage: the butterfly, the moon or full circle, the uninterrupted triangle are all symbols of immortality. The order of execution here, with one exception — the gold leaf pastaglia triangle — was background to middleground to foreground. The triangle was created first. The first painted area was the sky and the last to be painted was the butterfly. Underneath all this is a thoroughly rendered india ink underpainting of the middle to dark values.

THE DEATH OF EVENING STAR.

This clearly shows the close relationship between a scratchboard tool and a small pointed sable brush when both are used to linearly describe form. The difference between a scratchboard and an egg tempera is visually quite different. Nevertheless, the common denominator here is the linear approach to the resolution of form.

DREAM IN A CRYSTAL BALL *egg tempera on gessoed masonite 48" x 24" 1952 collection: Irma G. Harris, New Jersey*

Another of the early paintings that fall into the "man in fantasy" series. In most of these the form is warped out of expected representational imagery to enhance the overall rhythm and flow, also to project an "other world" idea called "fantasy".

SIX FISH — SILVER AND GOLD

egg tempera on gessoed masonite 24" x 30"
1949 collection: Joseph W. Wunsch, New York

Except for the six fish, the painting is largely flat tone and line. The fish are in low relief overlayed with gold and palladium leaf. The technique, known as *pastaglia*, is accomplished by building up the gesso where desired, carving out the form, and applying the metal.

North Light

a source book for artists

Marilyn Hafner

. . . she draws good

Marilyn Hafner

. . . she draws natural

. . . that's what I mean

I've been drawing ever since my father nailed a blackboard to my bedroom wall. I sold my first fashion drawing (2 views — 4 colors!) to my sister for 75¢ but since it was done on that blackboard her purchase had a certain ephemeral quality! I went on to fill in all the blank end papers in my books and when I began on the window shades, they sent me to Pratt to make an artist of me.

I wish I could combine nuggets of technical wisdom with startling insights into the Real World of the Creative Intelligence at work. But I can only say that I use a lot of felt markers, any paper available; and, yes, the life is hard!

I would rather be baking bread than meeting a deadline or doing 4-color separations; so, of course, between the procrastination and the desire to bill the job, I'm a nervous wreck!

I have done a wide range of graphic work during a career that began in high school. This covers fabric design, fashion illustration, layout, package design, magazine and advertising illustration and children's book illustration. I have come to the conclusion that there are no formulas, that every job requires a fresh viewpoint, and that newsprint tends to yellow!

My best work has been an enormous output of unsolicited mail: notes and letters, irritations, thank-yous, hellos, apologies, condolences and just plain communications. A sort of latter-day Samuel Pepys, my very life depends on the U.S. Post Office! These tiny works of "art" cover a major portion of the Western Hemisphere and of course are mostly lost to posterity. I say "mostly" — although there is a vast collection extant in Westchester County literally covering a wall belonging to a brother-in-law. My husband owns a unique bundle of notes, collages, drawings and 3-dimensional "things". Since these were done during our courtship, they are naturally too intimate for public view . . . a "private" collection indeed! Museums haven't the resources to track down this far-flung art form — although I have it on good authority that the principal graphics on the walls at Woman's Day Magazine are my manila-envelope-cat-drawings! My most faithful fans are the employees of the local Post Office. Once Mrs. Knight (Stamps & Parcel Post) told me that my envelopes "made her day" I was embarked on a life-long resolve to make her day forever! You may have guessed that I spend a lot of time in the Post Office. Now I no longer stand in line with the Public — I have my own place — south of Parcels — and I'm allowed to stamp "Special Delivery" myself so as not to ruin the design.

I can't enlighten young readers with a list of exotic materials and methods — like applying a mixture of titanium white and gull's droppings with the side of a sardine can and leave it out in the rain for six weeks!

I use — in addition to my beloved markers — rubber stamps, Victorian paste-on decals, torn paper, notary seals, crayon-pastels and ordinary pen and ink. Elegant illustration boards and fine papers intimidate me — so anything that comes to hand is o.k. Newsprint yellows — as I mentioned — tortillas tend to crack and bread dough molds — but any thin, cheap, easily-torn and folded paper does the job. A good mat improves everything. ▶

This drawing accompanied a very funny piece on living with a gourmet husband who leaves chaos in the wake of culinary masterpieces. My floor was covered with rejects before this one seemed to reflect the author's zany prose! The light-hearted mood and slapstick style called for a very spontaneous pen and ink drawing, with color indicated in felt markers. It was drawn directly — no preliminary pencil sketch — which uses up a lot of paper!

A page from "X Marks the Spot" (published by Coward-McCann-Geoghegan) which just won a Junior Literary Award. The color limitations here were 3 colors alternating with black and white. I used brush and ink and designer's gouache half tones throughout, so that on the color pages my overlays could achieve the effect of more than 3 colors. With a complete range of greys you can — with only one color overlay — get effects of a much larger color spectrum.

My thinking is visual, but my drawing is calligraphic and merely an extension of my concept — so the spontaneity of the sketch is the kernel of a successful drawing. In the past I've worked with creative art directors who have used my sketches for "finished" art. I feel that the idea **is** the finished art in a sense — the rendering for me is often the best way to kill a lively drawing.

I always get a great many visual ideas for a story, so the art director has a lot to choose from.

I'm glad to see that they are beginning to appreciate more variety of approach. In the '40's and '50's everything in magazines looked like it came out of one box. The only thing different was the format. In my early portfolio-lugging days the refrain was "Can't you make them prettier . . .?" "them" referring to the smiling children and suburban mums that I

draw for magazines. Now it's "Can't that be a bit uglier?". At least illustration is becoming innovative and esthetically interesting on its own. My commercial work fell into the pattern of what the art director wanted — my own expressions were confined to my very intimate communications. But happily, at last, it's beginning to be possible to fuse the two! I still draw a lot of smiling children and I **do** get a lot of visual ideas for illustrating pieces like "1000 Ways with Sour Cream" — but I do quite a bit of gardening between takes! When I get an assignment I read the manuscript and think about it for a long time. This allows me to keep up with the marketing and cooking and even bake an occasional loaf of bread. (My dream job would be to illustrate an enormous cookbook — having to prepare and consume each recipe.)

Then I begin visualizing ideas on paper, making small sketches that gradually get bigger as the concept begins to jell. And sometimes one of these larger sketches solves the problem at once and becomes the "finish" with only minor changes. The nicest thing about my small works and my humble materials is that you don't need a big studio or fancy cameras, lighting, etc.

I've done assignments at the picnic table on Cape Cod and even in the dark recesses of a restaurant! I love to see photographs of smiling successful artists wedged firmly between the parson's table and the light box, #10 flat sable in hand — complete with flourishing plants and Victorian antiques. This continues the mythical tradition of artist as noble beast — begun when the first painter posed in his velvet smock with the satin piano shawl over the easel. I worked in the corner of the bedroom (south light) for so many years that now even though I have a proper studio, I still tend to forage in a tight place under the work table.

I work from tangible references and unless absolutely necessary, I don't use photographic scrap. My files are a disaster. For years my three little girls were the kids I drew, and even now my cats, plants, furniture, husband and friends appear in my drawings.

In book illustration, the direct sketch-into-finish way of working is next to impossible — and I still haven't solved the problem of maintaining the spontaneity through the sheer working phases of dummies, color roughs, finished rendering and color separations.

I try to wrestle with this by making a **very** rough dummy so that the finished illustrations come as more of a surprise to me. If I have really digested the story and the concept is clear, the drawings or paintings should almost do themselves!

For me, the compensation for the frustrations, depressions and general hard times connected with being an artist is the real excitement of seeing something come out on the paper — sort of just appearing there! It's really magic!

How can you resist visualizing a nutty type in "mod" clothes after he has been "transformed" by the little woman from a creep in army pants and a shrunken sweatshirt? This was another funny vignette from life — meaning suburban life, where some subjects, like what your husband wears to a local fete, loom large. Somehow he looks familiar.

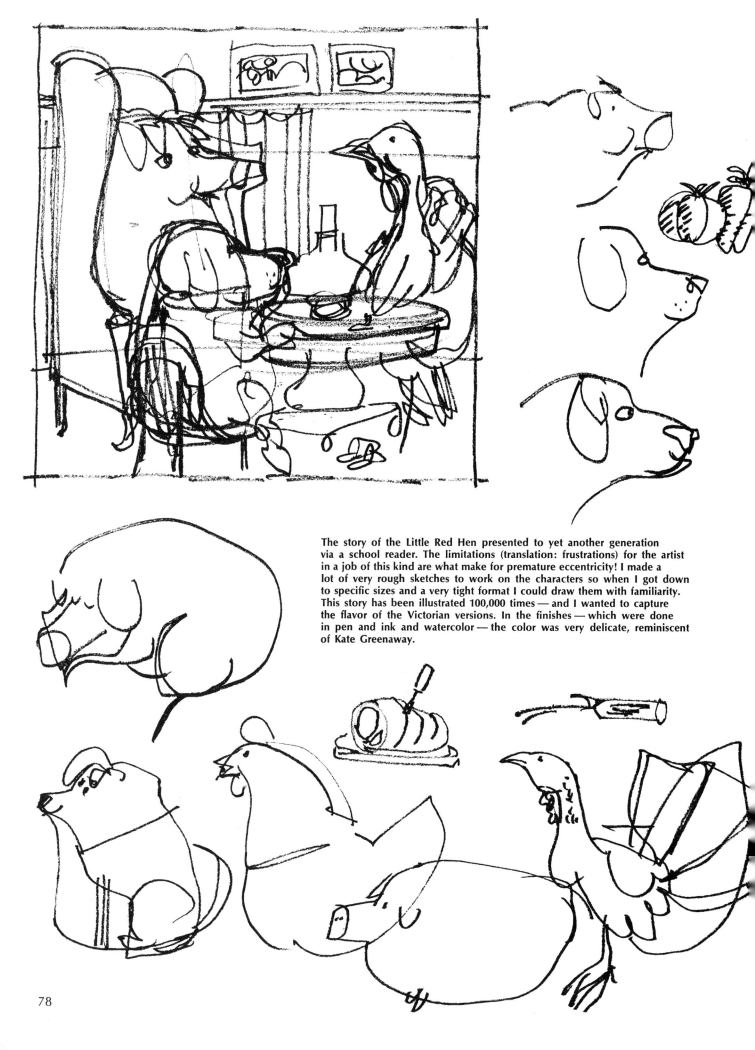

The story of the Little Red Hen presented to yet another generation
via a school reader. The limitations (translation: frustrations) for the artist
in a job of this kind are what make for premature eccentricity! I made a
lot of very rough sketches to work on the characters so when I got down
to specific sizes and a very tight format I could draw them with familiarity.
This story has been illustrated 100,000 times — and I wanted to capture
the flavor of the Victorian versions. In the finishes — which were done
in pen and ink and watercolor — the color was very delicate, reminiscent
of Kate Greenaway.

Kids: tan, small, fat, skinny, ugly and pretty have always been among my favorite subjects. My models were my own three girls and I imported boys from neighboring yards. I drew a monthly series on teen-agers for a few years.

Hand-Bone connected to the Funny-Bone

From 1946 to 1950 John Huehnergarth studied at the Museum College of Art in Philadelphia.

Since then a flood of imaginative drawings have flowed forth from his bottomless ink bottle.

Herewith, his views — and a small view of his ceaseless output.

PEOPLE WATCHING

I do a lot of it. I store it up like so many reels of movie film. As a kid my folks would pile us all into the family car, drive into the heart of Lancaster, Pa., where I grew up and just park along the curb and watch the shoppers go by on a Friday night. I might have begun people watching then or earlier, who knows, but I do know I enjoy watching what for me is the most interesting thing around — *the human being.*

I think most of us on this earth enjoy seeing and being seen. On a trip to the beach or to the Saturday night concert, the big attraction isn't always the sun, sand or symphony. It's the people — fat, skinny, short, tall and all. You watch them, they watch you. That's the way it is for me at any rate.

Into this mental file on people I inject a goodly amount of whimsy. That's essential for me. People shouldn't be taken too seriously — or life either for that matter — and a note of humor most always finds its way into my work. Sometimes my drawings are cartoons with an all out humorous slant while at other times a bitter or satirical note is sounded. At still other times, I use a designed or stylized approach in what I want the illustration to say. It depends a great deal on the material to be illustrated. In my desire to express the basic theme of the assignment, I try to have the art work accommodate to it.

Where watching people is concerned I do much the same. Watching someone I try to imagine what they feel inside and what motivates them. In an attempt to identify with the actions of another individual, I'm better able to remember his behavior and his corresponding figure movements. Later when the time comes to put it onto paper, the artist in us combines with the actor in us to momentarily step into the shoes of the individual we're illustrating.

It's important to me as an artist to tailor my illustrations to the material I'm illustrating. To me each assignment needs a special interpretation. That usually calls for a change in style from the last assignment and the technique is always chosen with the material to illustrate in mind.

An analogy to show business would not seem out of place in this regard. The artist needs to feel the mood of the material on hand and to develop a way of putting that mood on paper. He resembles an actor feeling out a new role.

Opening night, it might be said is when the pen or brush meets the paper. That stage fright upon facing the bright white footlights of the gleaming illustration board is familiar to most of us. But the artist brings to his performance all he can muster for the role. There's a bit of the actor in all of us they say. Well, in the case of an artist it helps if there's a whole ham. I feel that I act out a lot of Walter Mitty sort of fantasies in my work. For me, one of the advantages of people watching is the opportunity, even the necessity perhaps, of later acting out the person I was watching. Choosing the costume and the sets completes the picture. After all, isn't all the world a stage? We the actors?

However, no matter how important figures become to an illustration, the idea is the paramount element of a picture. Developing it can be a mysterious process. A very elusive one as well. A lot of the time I try as little as possible to analyze the procedure (if indeed there is one) for fear it'll become fretful at being withdrawn from my subconscious and leave in a huff altogether.

At times the harder I try for an idea the more blocked up it all gets. Brainstorming at times is like trying to see something better in darkness. Don't stare at it directly, but rather just above or below what you want to see. Real idea clarity for me is sometimes done in the same way. Give the brain an oblique approach, allowing time to weigh out all the ingredients — all mysterious, as I mentioned, but it works for me.

I work up tiny thumbnail sketches on scrap paper while I'm waiting for an idea to come along. More of a doodle than a sketch usually. I do them with a red grease pencil sometimes on the margin of a page of the manuscript or the back of an envelope. When an idea does arrive I usually go directly to the illustration board putting it down in light pencil prior to the follow-up inking. No real detail is done until the pen or brush work begins. Sometimes good supplementary ways to enhance the main idea occur while I'm doing the finished rendering and if they are strong enough I may even discard the first idea and go with one of the supplementary afterthoughts. If a preliminary sketch is required, the same procedure is followed except that the pencil replaces the pen in the finish of the rough sketch.

If an idea is particularly slow in coming, I have a method which I employ as a nitty gritty measure. I set out the illustration board itself on the drawing board and let it intimidate me. This contradicts the leave-your-mind-alone approach but there's a good and bad time for coddling and the latter method is good for producing an idea in an emergency.

Doing the actual art work is the icing on the cake. All the stops are pulled as the illustration comes alive beneath the pen. It's an experience that can be understood only by other artists. The translation of a mental image to paper is excitement hard to describe. The illustration itself reflects this feeling and conveys some of the emotion the artist experienced in doing it. It should also reflect the emotion set forth in the requirements of the assignment. Technique aids in setting a mood or elaborating on an idea and should be geared to the assignment itself.

My choice of styling or technique is largely inconsistent and follows no set pattern. In a single month I may work on a book, magazine cover, advertising campaign interchangeably switching styles like an actor changes costumes. I enjoy this variety and relish the change in pace it offers me. On with the show!

COVERS

Covers have been especially great. They offer more challenge usually and, of course to pass a newsstand and see them looking out at you is always a boost. *Newsweek* has bought the most from me in the cover department — twelve in the past ten years. Others run the gauntlet, ranging from *Jack & Jill* to the *New York Times Magazine*.

This **Newsweek** cover evolved from a conversation I had concerning the upcoming cover story with the economics editor. We thought showing the economy as a ponderous massive machine might be fun as well as an eye catcher. The machine part didn't really come to life as I developed my thinking on the subject. It was May 1970 and people were saying we were into a real recession. So I turned the machine into a structure or a "happening" and had the details spell out what was described by the article inside. This was first presented to the editors in sketch form. The important key to this assignment was coming up with an imaginative creation on which to hang the editorial comment.

Originally, when I did the sketch to show the editors, I thought that in order to demonstrate how it must feel to have all privacy stripped away one would need to be absolutely naked in the glare of all the watchful eyes. But, the more I thought about it, the more I felt it might lead to sex rearing its distracting head so I put clothes back on the subject couple. My object with all the foreboding equipment and menacing objects was to make the reader identify with that couple and feel threatened, too.

Here's an illustration of the El Conquistador Hotel in Puerto Rico where **Sports Illustrated** sent me to draw all the sporty types checking in. The place was capital "S" **sumptuous** and the people were some of the best subjects for people watching anywhere. The impression I wanted to make here was one that bespoke classy resort hotels and not too classy guests all in the same breath. The use of wash gives it more of a believable look.

The whole thing in this Holiday cover is the characterization of the different people. They all must come off as distinctly different types that might be opening up bank accounts. Line seemed a good way to keep it simple and dwell on the characters themselves.

In discussing the ideas for this **Time** cover, it was suggested that Kissinger might be rowing Nixon across to China, but I thought that looked a bit "slow-boat-to-Chinaish" and in a jet age we needed to chuck out the oars and get a sense of urgency into it. That clicked, and the whole thing seemed to benefit from the action. There wasn't time for a sketch or for full-color engraving, so flat color was used. Actually, pen and ink gave it a bit of an off-beat quality since almost all the covers are full-color.

A Gay Sultan? That's what the text called for in a book of gag one-liners for Simon and Schuster. To give it a fast-take kind of freshness, I used a brush throughout the book's illustrations.

Here's a nice, easy swing. You can feel that figure doing that action, but if you analyze it, he couldn't really be doing all that running, swinging the racket and lugging a suitcase. That's the beauty of carrying a cartoonist's license. **Sports Illustrated.**

For an article in **Life** about Red China, I felt the use of tiny figures to represent the millions of people was a natural. The suggestion of more figures than actually is drawn is sometimes possible by throwing them into perspective. The change in texture between the overbearing shadow of oppression and the pure line innocence of the masses is helpful in getting the point across.

To achieve the formal mood of this buffet party, black was used dominantly. You know at a glance it wasn't held in the afternoon. The extremely fragile line serves to heighten the contrast.

A lot of nicknames come up in sports circles, and that was the gist of the text for this **Sports Illustrated** illustration. If the name itself didn't imply whimsy, I put it there sometimes by only bugging out the eyes a little.

This is me. **Sports Illustrated** asked me for a drawing of myself for a short write-up and this was it. The supporting cast naturally was made up of sport types who aren't really riding me out of town on a rail.

In a story about Freud's shortcomings, the humor had to come from some sort of fantasy and dream-like contrivances. Sparked interest in reading the rather heavy text to show it in an off-beat way. In this case, Freud is shown viewing women's sexuality through a male model point of view.

Business Week needed a cover for an issue whose lead story was the mixed financial condition of the railroads used by the American commuters. So what better solution than to show one bright and punctual, and the other late and grimy. No sketch was made aside from the pencil put on the board prior to inking. The more I drew the more opportunity for contrasting situations seemed to come to mind.

When **Newsweek** asked me to do a drawing for the cover showing New York as a tough city to run, I figured the best solution would simply be to pack it with all the congestion which makes it that way. The more I drew, the more of a mess it became. Line with no embellishment seemed to leave more room for the details to jam in and give it a sort of fill-in color.

Out on the Salt Flats in Utah, I did drawings of a bunch of race car drivers for **Sports Illustrated.** It was hot and it was bright. The men were intense. I tried to get it all together in this one showing one driver demonstrating to another how he "spun out" on a turn of the track. Wash brought out the feeling of sun and salt.

At the time I did this, the plan was to show, on the cover, the promise of a bright future for the economic year with the prospect of a GNP of 700 billion in the offing. An obvious device was the bulging cash register and the skies raining dollar bills. Something very crucial to a cover design is having it read fast from a distance. The simplicity of the idea here helped that aspect of the design.

For this one on President Nixon's Phase II, a graphic backdrop of various shapes and colors suggested the grinding on of the ship of state with President Nixon at the controls. It was selected over two other pencil sketches submitted. The dilemma of the economy, as well as the complexities of it, is borne out by the strange, strained attitude of the President's figure.

The accompanying piece on Jack Levine
was written by Mr. Mahonri Sharp Young on
the occasion of his most recent exhibition
at the Kennedy Galleries in New York City.
We're grateful for its use and pleased to share
his enthusiastic views on this celebrated painter.

H. M.

JACK LEVINE

his work is represented in

herewith, are a few reasons why...

For Jack Levine The Figure Never Went Out. He paints the way the painted in the seventeenth century; it's not the only way to paint, but it the way the best work was done. He paints what Rembrandt painted. Ver few Americans have been able to handle the figure; most of them never trie or gave up early, like Morse. There has been a tremendous poverty progra in painting, and not just recently; what do we want to paint a bunch o flowers for, or a landscape?

Jack Levine was a prodigy, a *wunderkind* like Gericault; in the Fog there is a drawing he made at thirteen, like Durer's in the Albertina. Th gave him a tremendous start; he never had to learn to walk, he was alread running. Born in Berenson's Boston, he was always himself, and you coul pick out his work immediately. You see in his work what he sees in it him self; if you see ambiguity, he meant it that way. The son of a shoemake who had learned his trade in Russia, Levine really believes that painting related to manual skill; children of theoretical physicists, say, who do thei work in their heads, are not apt to be artists. He thinks that something passe between the eye and hand.

He studied with Harold Zimmerman from the time he was nine until h was sixteen, along with Hyman Bloom. This kind of thing, which happene in Vasari, is unheard of now. A real apprentice, he learned more than th teacher knew, and almost knew it beforehand.

This remarkably original artist had not one but two teachers. One da when he was hanging around the Boston Public Library with a portfoli under his arm, someone asked him what was in it. Levine drew him a coup' of sketches on library slips, which the man showed to Denman Ross. I those days, Ross was a famous man. Robert Henri and George Bellows, bot natural painters, thought his color theory was gospel truth. It sounds ma today, but why shouldn't there be a scientific basis? Every art school teach color theory, up to a point. They had theories on form too, like dynam symmetry; Arthur B. Davies thought he had discovered the secret of th Greeks.

Ross not only took on Levine as a pupil, he put him on the payroll, an then did the same for Zimmerman and Hyman Bloom. At fourteen, Levin had the run of the Fogg, with all the art in the world and a wonderful co servation department.

In the Thirties, people weren't buying many pictures, certainly not Jac Levine's. You can still see the drab winter cold in his work and the feelin with other people. He got on the Project, which was not the artistic glor we make it now, but it was a living.

When the War came, they got him. He did three and a half years, pa of it on Ascension Island, a fuel stop in the South Atlantic. Being an enliste man gives you an idea what it's like to belong to the criminal classes.

He didn't have much trouble getting back to civilian life. While he wa in the service, *The String Quartette* won a big prize at the Artists fc Victory exhibition at the Metropolitan, and he had saved part of his pa which is easy on Ascension. For quite a while, the Museum of Modern A had the idea that he was a modern artist, and then he started to sell whic he does not consider remarkable.

He used to draw a lot, but he is too shy to be a sketcher in the streets he hates being *the artist*. Everything he paints comes straight out of lif but it comes out in the studio. He goes to his studio six hours a day, si days a week, taking a sandwich with him. The way he paints takes a lor time. He works over and over, and keeps things for years. Some men now days can't paint until their show is about to open, and then they do it all once; how long does it take to paint a white line?

When he was young, there was an expressionist element in his work; admired Soutine and the early Kokoschka. But Soutine was a sick ma and some people had to do it with alcohol. Besides, the meaning went o of expressionism when it became abstract expressionism; there's a lot mo to Rembrandt than what we call reality. The only mystery is that there so much we can understand.

A thoroughly conscious painter, Levine believes in control. If you se political allusions in the smirks and funny hats, that's the way it is. He best at eyes and ears, he admits that, but he mainly paints the thought o the face. If his pictures have dramas and stories, that's what happens t people.

THE ROARING TROPICS – BOOM!, 1966-69, oil on canvas; 72 x 78 inches.

"I garbled the title from the song 'Night and Day'.

A shimmer of human tissue sharply punctuated by bits of bikini, beach chairs and parasols, I dealt with the Renaissance problem of intertwined nudes in color and light, in perspective and in concise geometric order. As Michelangelo said 'Serpentine, and multiplied by one, two and three.'

But for what Frank Jewett Mather termed 'athleticism' I substituted unathleticism."

WOMAN OF SINT OLAFSTRAAT, 1972, oil; 40 x 35 inches. Collection: The Artist

"Sintolof's is a street in the red light district of Amsterdam. The passerby will see on all sides large picture windows through each of which he will see a lightly clad woman seated in a cosily domestic living room.

As I painted this image my attention became focused on the one illuminated turquoise eyelid and the scarlet lipstick. The rest of the idea followed.

I ask myself why the street name remained in my head after many years. I suppose it's the apposition of saintliness and sin."

TEXAS DELEGATE, 1968-71, oil on canvas; 56 x 64 inches.

"An Austrian artist visiting me remarked on this image of the social villain as a departure from the 'fat rises' prototypes of Georg Grosz which have dominated protest painting ever since.

He felt this lean rawhide-tough cowboy was an American approach to the matter.

I don't know if they see the black hats riding on T.V. in Vienna, but I saw this man at the Democratic Convention of '68.

On a reddish sand colored base I tried to hold to red, white and blue as a color format."

SUSAN, 1967-72, oil on canvas; 32 x 28 inches.

"She is not my daughter as some have thought. My daughter's name is Susanna.

Susan is a winsome pretty girl. I am not known as a painter of winsome pretty images. But, as they say, 'Different folks, different strokes.'

This is why I am not an expressionist.''

THE NIGHT OF THE AVANT GARDE, 1969-71, oil on canvas; 78 x 72 inches. Private Collection.

"By now it seems the Avant Garde is the preserve of the middle-aged and the elderly. Youth seems to want no part of it.

In a nocturnal ambiance I looked for elements of foppishness and decrepitude. Two segments of the opera house keep reminding me of the tablets of Moses.

I have one of the leading authorities on American art sitting in a limousine in the background."

Tom, the *unswerveable* Lovell

In 40 years of picture making, Tom Lovell's approach has remained unchanged; a deep respect for fact — a devotion to historical accuracy and detail, and a total dedication to every canvas he sets before himself.

An old recipe begins, "First catch the rabbit." This logical priority should be followed by all historical painters. The viewer must be induced and persuaded by whatever means the artist can bring to bear, that something worth his attention is taking place.

My approach is to learn all I can about the subject, work out the strongest possible design and present it in such a way that "you are there." Part of this hinges on the ability to make people believable, not models dressed in costume. When Defoe recorded Crusoe's delight in finding another human being, he simply acknowledged man's need for and interest in his own kind. This fundamental and unremarkable trait finds its application in my work. I like people, and the countless variations of face and form are a very real part of the visual world. If I can communicate some of this feeling in each painting, common ground may be established with the casual spectator who brings nothing more to the subject than his own interest in mankind. Some clam diggers move along the shore; from a distance their faces are not visible, but I am interested in what they are doing. They make the picture. On my easel there stands a half-finished painting of a group of Lipan Apaches under a cottonwood tree. The year is 1535. I don't know as much about them as I wish, but enough to tell the story. If they rolled up their tule mats and moved away, most of my interest in the place would go with them.

In picture making of this kind, I believe the artist has a certain obligation to interest and inform without being encyclopedic about detail. Exact costumes, weapons, artifacts, etc. are usually impossible to come by; in such cases the artist must rely on his general knowledge and picture sense. Rented props are fine if available, but I prefer having half a dozen good plates of a military great-coat of 1855 than a present-day approximation of the garment provided by the costumer, usually several sizes too small. Along with a scattering of bonifide period weapons, I undoubtedly have the finest collection of homemade cardboard and wooden swords, armor, battle-axes, crossbows, etc. in New England, and these fragile relics have earned their keep over and over again.

In 1968 I travelled through Sweden, Norway, Denmark, England and Ireland to research a series of paintings on the Vikings for National Geographic Society.

As a preliminary I spent two months reading all available material and making comprehensive color sketches; these became the basis of talks, first with the editorial people in Washington, and later with various experts and curators abroad. I have found such conversations are more fruitful when based on something tangible.

Convincing representations of ships of by-gone days call for technical information usually not obtainable. I often make models to solve these problems. The Viking trading ship is a case in point. In the picture the vessel was seen in perspective, partly aground at low tide, as a work party unloaded cattle and household gear. Having visited the Maritime Museum at Roskilde, Denmark and seen the half-finished reconstruction of a similar ship, I knew the basic proportions. I learned a good deal about the method of construction from visits to other museums and much reading. Three and a half days later I saw the model completed with partly lowered yard and sail, plus figures for scale; the hull was placed at a correct list in a cut-out opening in a cardboard sea. I had most of the information I needed before me.

Two other models were made for the same Viking series; these were rough water-line hulls, but with complete sails and standing and running rigging. Handling my sloop on Long Island Sound supplied the practical experience.

Important as such technicalities are, they must remain subordinate to the demands of composition and design, and to the key roll played by people, the common denominator between past and present.

As a veteran illustrator, I have done my share of the contemporary scene, but I enjoy re-creating the past. As a boy, books of adventure in far off times and places were as real as the sand lot football game after school, or the week-end hike of Troop 8 to Great Notch, N.J. At seventeen I shipped as a deckhand on the fabled Leviathan and had a taste of the North Atlantic in winter. Various other jobs followed; caddy master at a golf club, messenger for Wright Aero Corp., and time keeper for several hundred men working for a construction company. All this was grist for the mill; and, by the process of elimination, I came to some conclusions about things I did not want to do for a living. Though I had no contacts with artists, the world of books and museums and pictures looked brighter

than ever, so enrollment in the College of Fine Arts, Syracuse University was the next step. A kindly providence directed that my four years at Syracuse be devoted largely to figure and portrait painting. Experience in composition was gained in a more practical way. At this time the newsstands were filled with "pulp" magazines devoted to action, adventure and mayhem; these lurid vehicles offered an ideal training ground for the young illustrator. I was able to find such work in the summer of my junior year and produced a cover in oils and eight or ten dry-brush illustrations each month during my senior year.

The miniscule rate of pay (seven dollars a full page drawing) precluded the use of models and obliged the artist to learn to draw from the mirror or do without. It was an ideal way to learn composition. The dry brush drawings were reproduced on poor stock and depended little on a middle tone; the picture story had to be told with the greatest economy of means and at small scale. It was a question of boiling down and closing in on the subject; even more so on the covers because their message had to "carry" i.e. out-scream a hundred others. Full length figures seldom appeared, except in cases of victims rigged horizontally for torture or worse.

After graduation I continued to free-lance for the pulps for six years before tackling the "slicks". Serials by Edna Ferber, Louis Bromfield, Paul Gallico, Sinclair Lewis and others came my way and the chance to depict period as well as character and action.

In 1944 I enlisted in the Marine Corps with the objective of serving as a combat artist. After Parris Island I was assigned to the staff of Leatherneck Magazine and fought the rest of the war at an easel, to the relief of my family. A great opportunity existed here to portray the Marine Corps past and present, and my first large scale historical paintings were done in dungarees along side my painter friend John Clymer, whose serial number stood one digit below mine. (This probably made us the only two characters out of Boot Camp who remembered another guy's number.) Some of these paintings now hang in Marine Corps Headquarters and various parts of the Capitol.

Illustration continued to flourish after the war, and with fiction assignments there were subjects that included military events, exploration, and adventures on land and sea based on historical facts.

Joli

The first use of Prof. Lowe's balloon as an observation point in the Civil War was certainly a milestone, yet a close-up of the now familiar shape did not seem a promising solution. Instead I chose the human element, Confederate troops trying (vainly) to shoot it down.

Obviously, cumulative experience plays a part in the handling of masses of figures. Alexander's troops coming ashore in Asia Minor have much in common with the Second Marine Division at Tarawa. Earlier assignments of Civil War subjects gave me opportunity to take part in Life Magazine's series on the occasion of the Centennial in 1961. The wide range of subjects for the National Geographic Society included Abraham, the ancient Greeks, The Vikings, William the Conqueror and his Normans, Spanish Treasure Ships, and Appomattox Court House.

In recent years I did a series of paintings for the Mormon Church, two of these being the largest pictures I have done. All were concerned with its early history. The cordial reception accorded these works has given me a sense of accomplishment far beyond the ordinary exchange of client and artist.

There is no substitute for first-hand knowledge, but the painter is denied this luxury in most cases, though there are compensations. For example, one of the Civil War assignments required a painting of the Federal Fleet passing before the batteries at Vicksburg. After reading the logs of the vessels involved, and moving small scale models along a table top against a backdrop drawing of the city, I probably had a better understanding of exactly what took place that night than anyone involved in the action, either in a shore battery or a ship.

To do full justice to his subject, the artist must have the widest possible knowledge of his material so that he may be able to present the heart and spirit of the matter in one go. He is denied the leisurely approach, build-up, and multiple opportunity afforded by other mediums of communication, e.g. the writers' craft or film making. The epic approach is always a prime consideration, yet within this framework a final decision eventually must be made to settle on a given moment with the hope that it is the right one.

The indebtedness of the traditional painter to others is considerable by definition. How could the Greek troops at the siege of Tyre be properly represented without first making an exhaustive study of the figures so beautifully delineated on their vases? I admire and have been helped by the work of many men; the tremendous innovations made by the Impressionists; also Sargent, Sorolla, Zorn, Remington, Russell, Pyle, Dunn — a long list of household gods with no proper end. Years ago Don Teague and Meade Schaeffer each gave me a hand up at just the right moment; Harold Von Schmidt by suggestion and example continues to inspire to this day, and the same can be said of Bob Lougheed and John Clymer, though, alas, at a distance, both having moved west.

In 1970 I accepted a commission to execute a series of historical paintings for a foundation in the Southwest, the canvases eventually to be displayed permanently in a museum. This work is still in progress. The subjects are complex for the most part, requiring research in depth and sometimes trips to locations for data on the character of soil, rock, vegetation, as well as trips to Museums. My wife Gloyd and daughter Deborah, both artists, often go along on these junkets, making life more pleasant and, not incidentally, expanding my note and sketch-making potential three-fold.

In short, things I liked as a boy are still appealing to me, and I am able to do something about it. My home is on a hill overlooking Long Island Sound; and as I watch the water and the sky, I think of the real old-timers, the Indians who lived in this same spot, drank from my little spring and generally went about their business. Like them, I am simply a custodian, and for me the place is better for the recollection of former times. I hope some of this is found in my work.

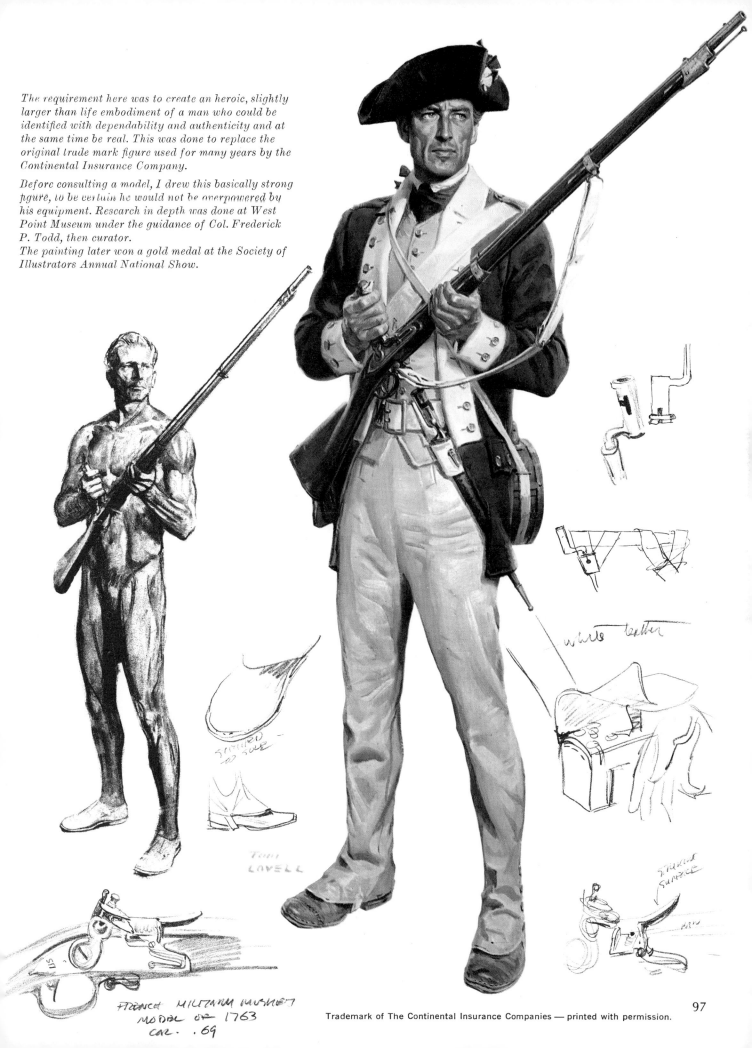

The requirement here was to create an heroic, slightly larger than life embodiment of a man who could be identified with dependability and authenticity and at the same time be real. This was done to replace the original trade mark figure used for many years by the Continental Insurance Company.

Before consulting a model, I drew this basically strong figure, to be certain he would not be overpowered by his equipment. Research in depth was done at West Point Museum under the guidance of Col. Frederick P. Todd, then curator.

The painting later won a gold medal at the Society of Illustrators Annual National Show.

Tom LOVELL

FRENCH MILITARY MUSKET
MODEL OR 1763
CAL. .69

97

Essentially a portrait of Thoreau he is seen at Walden Pond building his cabin. In character, though holding a borrowed axe, his concern and delight is with nature, not work. Showing the partly finished cabin could only have detracted from the duet of man and nature.

The S.S. Laurentic, carrying gold for Canada, was sunk off the Irish coast in World War I. The ensuing salvage operation was a model of efficiency and courage, with much of the work done under adverse weather conditions. I tried to show the wild power of the sea, the diver struggling up the ladder as the vessel rolled heavily under a rising wind, all in as close compass as possible.

I tried to place the observer in the middle of the battle of Hastings. Bishop Odo on his white horse makes the crest of the wave of Normans that break against Harold's wall of shields. Later the action became scattered, offering less opportunity for a closely organized composition.

I usually plan my pictures in small roughs to establish pattern, movement and placing of figures, then go to a full size cartoon done either on brown wrapping paper or draughtsman's paper that takes charcoal and punishment. Here I experiment with refinements of action without use of models, as seen in this Viking feast, leaving the drawing unfixed. Then I take photographs and redraw where necessary. Basic outlines of this cartoon are then transfered with home-made carbon (charcoal) paper to the canvas, exercising options of placing and proportion up to the last.

The site of Leif's Vinland has never been established, so after much sketch making and discussion, the later landing of the Karlsefni expedition at Epaves Bay in Newfoundland was decided on. Objective was to show as much as possible of the people, their gear, cattle and ships, in a notable, but non-heroic moment in history. Reproduction appeared in April 1970 issue of National Geographic M

Viking long-ships have been pictured many times, but they probably did not come to the new world and certainly not with Karlsefni It was important that the portrayal of these vessels be as authentic as possible, hence the model, made of wood, cardboard, glue and love, not necessarily in that order.

I frequently draw from the mirror for information on hands, faces, bits of drapery etc. as the work progresses. Members of the family are sometimes pressed into service, as in the case of the slave girl, to study the folds of a garment in an electric fan breeze.

ARTIST on the SPOT

When you start to draw people and portraits, it's natural to pick people who don't move, like statues or sleeping babies. I added the toys here as it seemed part of Michelle's world. It took a trip around the house to find and draw them, but I'm grateful to her for supplying the subject matter. It tells the viewers more about the person being portrayed.

NORMAN MacDONALD

Meet a young Canadian artist, now living in Amsterdam, Holland, whose international clients send him on drawing assignments around the world. Here, he discusses his philosophy and approach to drawing and painting.

The drawings on this page were made in approximately one hour. It's an exercise in drawing people in movement. There are no rules other than to draw as quickly and carefully as possible, a test requiring all your attention. The purpose is to train your eye to catch and hold a gesture. The exercise is also to remember the gesture so that you can finish it after the person has gone on to do something else.

Aperson's approach to drawing has to be an extension of himself, an individual way of thinking and living. It should be as natural as writing one's name. Although I have a farily good idea what I want to accomplish when beginning a drawing, I try to let things happen as I proceed. Unexpected changes and developments have had the greatest influence on my work.

I draw the way I live. "Fate" influences my final product more than any planned effort. Not that I sit around and wait for things to happen — I have as many goals as the next person and work hard to reach them. But my original plan is formed only to increase the chances of coincidence, to save time and to avoid fumbling.

In my opinion, good art is better today than in any other period in the past.

I think artists today have stopped worrying about being classicists, romanticists, impressionists, cubists or "ists" of any kind. The worthy artist is simply trying to be himself!

This is not to say that one should ignore the past — it would be folly not to take advantage of the knowl-

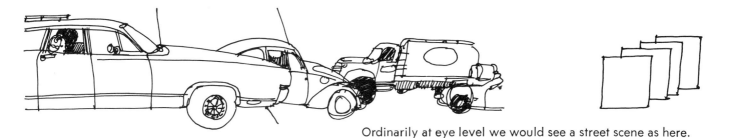

Ordinarily at eye level we would see a street scene as here.

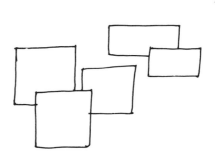

If you give story telling more importance than perspective, as in this drawing, you are able to show or tell more about the subject.

In this drawing I wanted to bring all the ingredients of city life into the drawing, especially the movement. Movement doesn't have to be observed at 1/500 of a second. You can take your time and study it over a period of time. This will give you a chance to design it the way you want, and not be forced to accept the action at a fraction of a second.

104

edge and discoveries of the great talents that have gone before us. But one should remember that the great ones were **individuals.** They absorbed the best of what went before them — then spent their lives emerging as **themselves.**

This is my aim also — I worship the best of the past — but I don't blindly accept **all** the past simply because it's old. And I'm afraid many people do: witness how many museums and collectors acquire works of art as they might antiques — simply because they're old and novel. And when the media report the acquisition of a rare work they seldom dwell on its artistic worth — only its monetary value. Art talk should differ from Wall Street talk.

I spend a great deal of time in museums and I recommend museum study for several reasons, partly as a way of keeping humble — but more importantly because it's a kind of religion.

When we study 15th Century religious works, we see the artists' storytelling ability and also marvel at their methods of communicating — whether painting on walls or panels.

This shows how the drawing fits together.
You can see that movement can't be
simply accepted. Planning is essential.

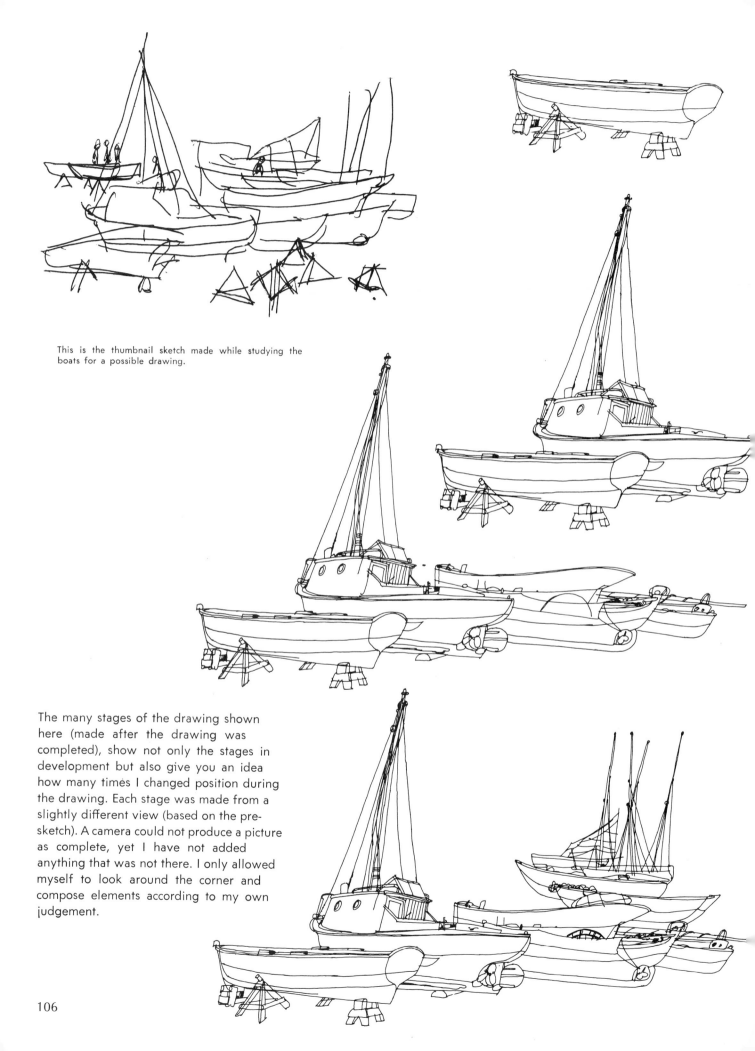

This is the thumbnail sketch made while studying the boats for a possible drawing.

The many stages of the drawing shown here (made after the drawing was completed), show not only the stages in development but also give you an idea how many times I changed position during the drawing. Each stage was made from a slightly different view (based on the pre-sketch). A camera could not produce a picture as complete, yet I have not added anything that was not there. I only allowed myself to look around the corner and compose elements according to my own judgement.

Between this stage and the final drawing,
I concentrate more on the drawing than the
subject. With the objects being well
established, the problem is to complete
the picture according to the rules of picture
making. Values, Textures and people are
added to give variety and balance to
the lines and shapes of the boats.

To me, drawing might be a meaningless exercise if I couldn't use it to record the world around me. The world I record is different from your world. Our private little worlds help each of us to create a personal identity. This is becoming increasingly important in an era of mass production and standardization. To observe and record goes beyond the point of proficiency, although this is very important in the beginning. I believe art begins where proficiency leaves off and from this point on we are susceptible to our true inner selves. What we believe or observe we can state more surely. This has been called by many names: confidence, professionalism, talent or just "your thing." Being close to our thing, it is impossible to escape that which interests us more than it does others.

Having special interests is both natural and advantageous. Having an obsession to draw our special interests really means being a bit of an egomaniac. All artists possess this to some degree. Once, while watching speakers at Hyde Park in London on Sunday morning, it struck me that artists have a lot in common with soap box orators. They have to comment on subjects (good or bad).

Belmonte Castle
La Mancha Spain

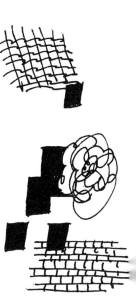

In this drawing I realized how important black areas are when used in combination with other textures.

Color

Any mediums which belong to the category of paint, I put under the title of color. I can't separate one type of paint from another because I sometimes use several in one picture. When I begin with watercolor, however, I like to stick with it throughout the whole painting.

My usual procedure is to paint until I get a certain value pattern set up. Then I get to the point where I start backing up and lightening some colors and then begin working on the darker values. This is best done with acrylics. You can thin the paint to the consistency of watercolor or thicken it so it resembles oil paint from the tube.

This medium also is fast drying and can be used on any surface. Sometimes I like to add crayons for texture or watercolor for glazes at this stage. I usually try to create the darkest values with pencil because I can do this gradually until I'm satisfied.

Another way I darken values is glazing with washes until the color has reached the right value.

When I work outdoors
I make color notes and
apply the paint later.

Bodensea, Konstanz Switzerland

There are no rules as to when to draw. The time is when you are motivated. It's nice when familiar things close to you still move you to draw. It means you are still keen on the subject or at least not taking it for granted.

The medium here is a combination of watercolor, acrylics and poster paint over a pencil drawing on d'Arches watercolor paper (640 g). The water was the most difficult area. Before I had the right value I had squeezed out three tubes of cobalt blue.

North Light®
. . . a source book for artists

Photo by Bill Noyes

The good
word "creative"
is misused
and misplaced
more often
than any
other in
art circles.
It should be
applied
sparingly.
Here it's
applied
knowingly.
McDermott
can do
anything he
sets his
hand to.
And he does
it with skill
and affection
all his
waking hours.

112

Need a man to make a movie....paint a picture.... write a book? Try John McDermott. He specializes in *everything*.

THE MOST FAMOUS ARTIST I almost met was the Montana cowboy painter, Charlie Russell.

I was five years old and tearing up the track in kindergarten when the well-meaning teacher showed some of my drawings to the ailing Mr. Russell. He said what artists usually say (if they have any manners) about the work of hyperactive midgets and everyone was grateful. He died a year later, fortunately never knowing what he had encouraged.

Russell did (however unknowingly) exert a strong influence over my feelings about pictures and the direction I would take. A great many of his originals hung in bars and offices around Great Falls, Montana, where we lived, and I must have been shown them all. The message was not lost on a small boy. It was perfectly OK for a real artist to draw horses, cowboys and Indians. Or even pirates fighting to the death on yellow moonlit beaches while armed tough guys watched from the ragged palms. Adult-approved melodrama! I was sold.

Howard Pyle's Book of Pirates was a Christmas gift before I could read and still have the copy with my name in romper-school hieroglyphics on the fly leaf to prove it.

I began drawing at about 4. There were grandmotherly complaints about having to sharpen all those pencils but I had to get down all that black smoke pouring out of those flaming pirate ships.

At the age of 6, having exhausted Montana (and my grandmother) I was summoned to Hollywood. Not by MGM but by my mother. Riding down Hollywood Boulevard from the LA station, I actually saw Ben Turpin and company shooting a two-reeler on the sidewalk. My love-hate relationship with films began. Growing up, I spent spare Saturdays climbing the fences at Fox, Metro and the old Ralph Ince lot to stare at the sets. I practically memorized the battered French village from "The Big Parade" and the idea of a full-masted sailing ship sticking up out of the eucalyptus trees still moves me. In grade school I was, like all artists, the "best drawer" in class. My teacher in the 3rd grade was John Ford's sister (another close call with fame!) and a very pleasant permissive woman. She decided I should spend most of my time drawing. Thus it was I escaped learning arithmetic and, since I eventually entered the commercial art field, have never missed it much, particularly "addition."

About this time I discovered the great material hiding out in history books and I sat copying pictures out of those oversized volumes while the rest of the drones studied. While they learned the multiplication tables, I smeared away at Cortez raising hell in Mexico and the Light Brigade falling off its horses at Balaclava. Horrible as it sounds, I was copying some excellent academic draughtsmen and actually learned something here and there.

In "art class" I was the despair of the art teachers because of my "brush techniques". I applied color as if I was cleaning the brush on the painting surface. I don't know whether their beef had to do with esthetics or economy but I stuck to my guns and I still wear out an extraordinary number of brushes on a job.

As a standard pathologically-shy adolescent, I approached good-looking girls by way of that con job known to all artists, the "portrait". Unable to say much more than "Hi," I could thus spend time in their magic presence and show off a bit at the board. Those were strange portraits. The resemblances were passable but the subjects looked ominously healthy. All skin tones glowed with second degree sunburn verging on apoplexy. I hadn't yet heard about cool colors.

I was also copying Greta Garbo off the cover of Photoplay regularly and nearly caught up to Earl Christy a couple of times. Max Baer I lifted from Salvador Baguez drawings in the sports pages. He was a genius at pencil techniques that are rediscovered every few years in the commercial game. At that time, pastels were my medium and there was always a faint cloud of orange dust in the air.

Graduating high school, I went to work at 17 for Walt Disney studios. In my family, art schools were for rich kids. At Disney's I did meet a number of fellow prisoners who *had* studied and, bored crazy by Mickey and Donald and Goofy, we went painting landscapes on weekends and occasionally hired a model. I was taken aside at last by one quiet spoken fellow who could no longer stand my palette and told me all about Ultramarine Blue and Alizarin Crimson and Viridian Green. The results were electrifying. The portraits caught a cool highlight now and then. All this time I had assumed Burnt Umber was "hair color" and Cadmium Red was "lip".

In the Marines as a combat artist, I traveled with the troops and for three years got all the drawing opportunity anyone could want. My work changed enormously during this time and I'm sure it was due to constant drawing every single day from life. No photographs, no copying somebody's historical painting. Just putting down what I saw around me. In a few instances it was a dangerous kind of scholarship, but it was the nearest I ever had to an unrelieved stint of drawing.

When I got out I knew I wouldn't return to Dippy Dog so I came to NY to be an illustrator. Just like that. Looking back, it's fortunate I didn't know any better because for several years I was about an eighth

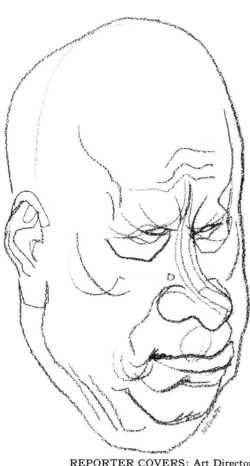

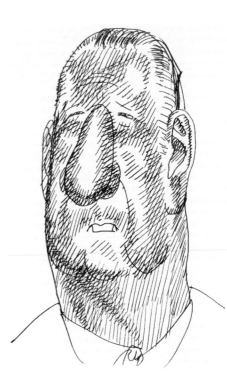

These were done for fun, used by "Reporter". They are a kind of nervous doodling that goes on constantly. A good character analysis exercise.

REPORTER COVERS: Art Director Reg Massie allowed total freedom for the artist. Any errors here are my own. Reg would suggest a subject some times but that is as far as he ever approached "control". In its time, as a result of his policies, "The Reporter" carried the best covers (not these by any means) of any commercial magazine. "The Reporter" is missed badly. Reg is currently A.D. of Gourmet.

PAGES FROM BELLEAU WOOD SHOOTING SCRIPT:
Scenes were envisioned in thumbnails first and shot to the pencilled compositions. Particular filters were listed beside the scene as well as the angle of the sun correct for that time in the story. Zoom shots and all camera movements necessary to the story were blocked out on the compositions. The finished picture was thus spared lots of unrelated scenes and spectacular unusable footage. Pick-up shots (that looked "great" at the time but weren't in the script) invariably looked miserable when cut into the reel. This control is one discipline I swear by. Ad libbing is vastly overrated when an audience is growing restless to the point of murder and the film is still floundering in self-indulgent spontaneity.

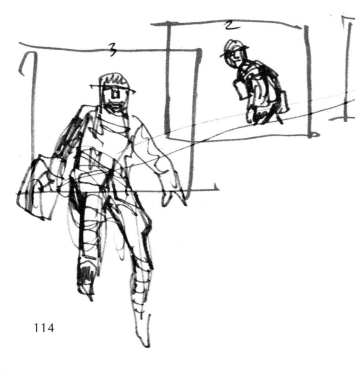

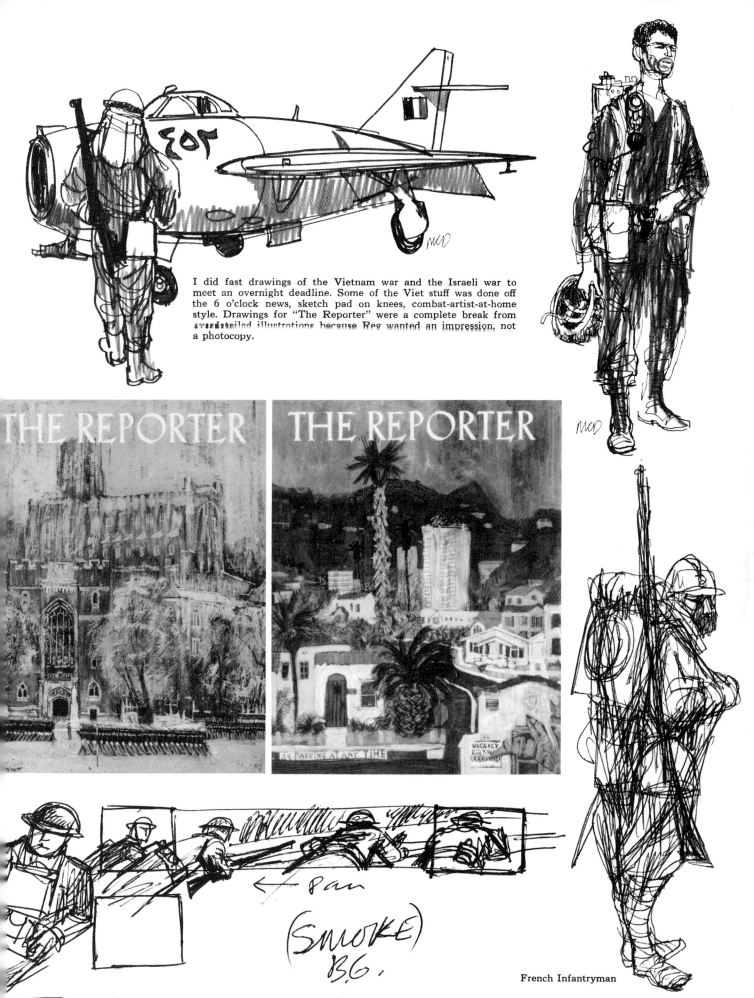

I did fast drawings of the Vietnam war and the Israeli war to meet an overnight deadline. Some of the Viet stuff was done off the 6 o'clock news, sketch pad on knees, combat-artist-at-home style. Drawings for "The Reporter" were a complete break from detailed illustrations because Reg wanted an impression, not a photocopy.

THE REPORTER

THE REPORTER

NO PARKING AT ANY TIME

NO VACANCY

← Pan

(SMOKE) B.G.

French Infantryman

of an inch away from starvation. Because I never worked in a studio and freelanced from the start, I had to teach myself how to paint illustrations.

I've been attracted to miniatures from a very early age and made a great many scale models to work from in my illustrations. Cars, ships, planes and buildings thus could be photographed in the exact lighting I wanted. And they saved me several years of mechanical drawing, something I always found to be sheer torture.

Also a lifelong movie nut, I began making my own in 16mm sound. (With the help of a few hundred of my friends) I wrote the scripts, thumbnailed the scenes ahead of time for some sort of final coherence, operated the camera, cut the film and dubbed the sound.

I made scale models of props we couldn't get, such as Civil War artillery and wagons. For the Battle of Antietam film, I built a scale model of the Dunker Church from the original plans loaned me by the National Park Service and the model is now a display at the battlefield site in Sharpsburg, Maryland. The models were photographed with wide-angle lenses to increase perspective and always with live figures in the same frame. Scriptwriting led to my first novel. I've published four novels (one of which was "adapted" for "Loving", with George Segal and Eva Marie Saint) and made a total of seven films. One of these, "Pickett's Charge" ran on CBS network twice.

To me, painting, writing and making films are merely different means of achieving the same result — the communication of an idea. An illustration must say it all in one picture; a novel can take chapters and build toward a finish; a film is a happy combina-

A Marine BAR man on Okinawa was firing at a Japanese machine gun emplacement when one of the bad sports tossed a grenade at him. Part of the fight for Shuri and Wana Ridge in May, 1945. The dead Japanese soldier (right) was killed by artillery fire in the town with the appropriate name of Makabe on southern Okinawa. Dead-man drawings were not released by HQ during the war and I kept these sketches of mine to remind anyone interested that it wasn't all John Wayne.

PORTRAIT OF RUTH:
Acrylics. Was done to work up a sort of 1900 style for a job in the works. Heated objections to the background which is interior of the station wagon in which we spent the best years of our lives. It will look alright in 100 years when the station wagon will be known as the buckboard of its time.

tion of all of it — pictures, story line, cutting for effect and sound. I always found the three fields to be not all that far apart.

In time, however, the films proved so expensive and 16mm facilities so frustrating that I confine myself now to sparetime novels and fulltime painting.

My own conclusions about painting tend to be mercifully few and are as contrary and as contradictory as the subject itself. "Rules are made to be broken" seems a good general idea and "Don't listen to anybody" is balanced nicely by "Learn everything you can". I think this last is a safe idea because I doubt very much if anyone ever really learns very much about it. Of course there are artists who are sure they know upwards of 90% of what there is to know about painting but that must remain their problem.

The whole thing is too illusory. That vision in your mind is always just beyond you.

And that, of course, is what keeps it interesting.

Done for myself from a longtime interest in boxing. Used to illustrate magazine article. At one time it was to be used for "Requiem For A Heavyweight". Thank God I didn't change the guy's face to look like Anthony Quinn because the deal collapsed and I still have my picture with no moviestar distortions.

Painted on Guadalcanal, 1945, oil on plywood. Would be there still but for a broadminded pilot who saw no reason why he couldn't fly it back to Washington on a transport plane after all the brass had given up. I wanted to paint three types I felt were typical of the Mar Corps I saw in the Pacific and called it "Three Marines". After appearing on a book jacket, it was known as "The Long And The Short And The Tall" which shows what can happen to an innocent idea. The painting hangs in the Commandant's office at USMC headquarters, which is as near as I got to winning the Congressional Medal of Honor, a semi-secret dream of mine.

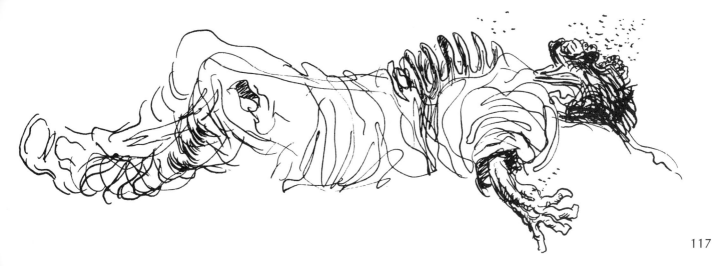

117

Bonaparte was known for his itch, a fantastic break for me. Otherwise the picture might have been a field of pink bubbles or purple scratches. As is my custom when hooked by a subject, I tried to include the entire world in the picture but narrowed it down to a few flags and several of his most noted regiments. The most interesting assignment in about forty years.

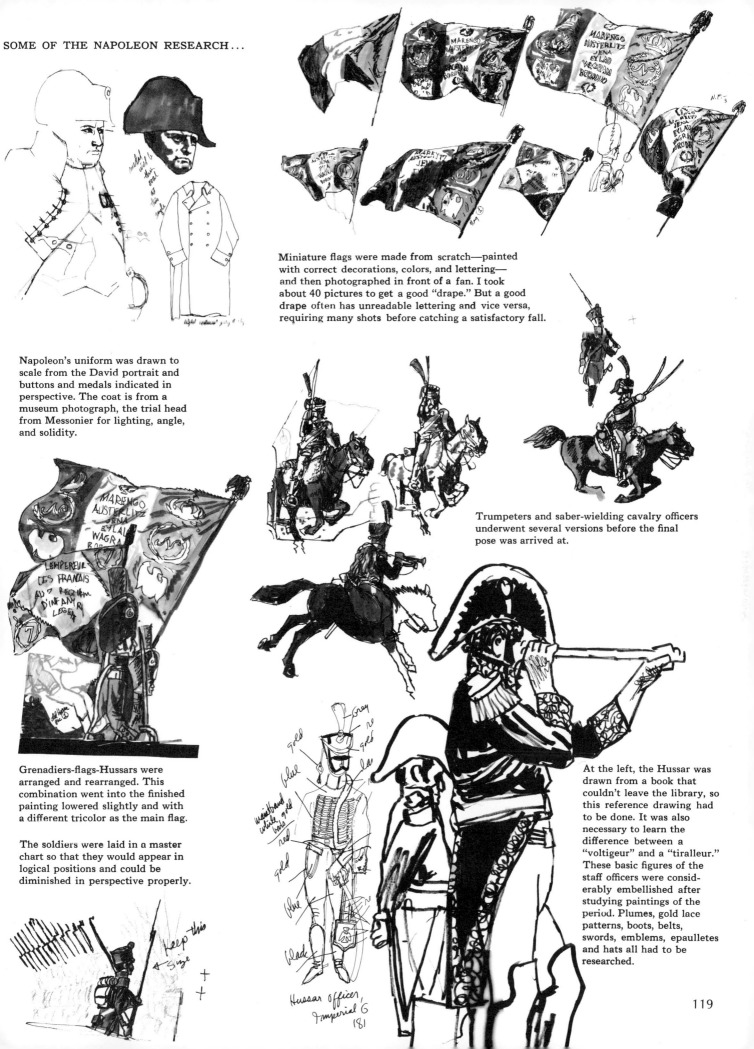

SOME OF THE NAPOLEON RESEARCH...

Miniature flags were made from scratch—painted with correct decorations, colors, and lettering—and then photographed in front of a fan. I took about 40 pictures to get a good "drape." But a good drape often has unreadable lettering and vice versa, requiring many shots before catching a satisfactory fall.

Napoleon's uniform was drawn to scale from the David portrait and buttons and medals indicated in perspective. The coat is from a museum photograph, the trial head from Messonier for lighting, angle, and solidity.

Trumpeters and saber-wielding cavalry officers underwent several versions before the final pose was arrived at.

Grenadiers-flags-Hussars were arranged and rearranged. This combination went into the finished painting lowered slightly and with a different tricolor as the main flag.

The soldiers were laid in a master chart so that they would appear in logical positions and could be diminished in perspective properly.

At the left, the Hussar was drawn from a book that couldn't leave the library, so this reference drawing had to be done. It was also necessary to learn the difference between a "voltigeur" and a "tiralleur." These basic figures of the staff officers were considerably embellished after studying paintings of the period. Plumes, gold lace patterns, boots, belts, swords, emblems, epaulletes and hats all had to be researched.

119

ALVIN PIMSLER:
doer of dudes in fancy duds ... and other things

He has long been known as a leading Men's Fashion artist. What is just now being discovered is that he has also developed into a painter of scintillating alive portraits. Herein, are his thoughts on both pursuits.

Photographed by Bill Jolie in the work rooms of Saks Fifth Avenue, N.Y.C.

I'm one of those fortunate people whose early interest in drawing was encouraged by my parents. They urged me to study art as a profession. My awareness until the time I went to art school was on a very simple level; I had only a superficial acquaintance with painting and the history of art. However, I did know something about the commercial field, particularly that part of it that had to do with retail advertising done by department and speciality stores. This information came from an uncle to whom I was very close. He had been trained as an architect, but somehow had gravitated into this field and done extremely well doing drawings of fashion accessories. Macy's, Altman's, Lord & Taylor and mail order houses like Sears and Penny's all used his work. He was always busy and turned out a phenomenal amount of stuff. I ran errands for him and spent the time in between watching him work.

After my first year at Pratt Institute, I had to decide which special field of advertising design or illustration to concentrate on. My uncle suggested men's fashion, which he said was a lucrative and not particularly crowded field. These were days when the great depression was still touching people, so "making a living" was something we all thought about. So, even though I didn't have a foppish interest in clothes, his reasoning appealed to me and I decided to plunge.

The Fashion Illustration course offered then concerned itself only with women, so actually I had to find my own way. Mostly I watched the ads as they appeared in the daily papers and tried to emulate them. In addition, I added men and sought more dramatic and original approaches. I also spent a great deal of time doing posters and advertising design problems.

After graduation I was offered a job as an apprentice in a men's fashion studio, but I turned it down because there was no pay offered. **None whatsoever.** (Uncle, oh Uncle!) However, a short time later I landed a job with the Herald Tribune in the promotion department doing a little of everything. Next came a great opportunity to join the hot art department of Bamberger's in Newark. It was for a great deal less money, but I took it gladly. It was there that I really began to learn men's fashion. Morris Rosenbloom and his art department were recognized as doing the best retail advertising in the U.S. "Rosie" believed in taking young people just out of school, and bringing them along at their own pace, giving them more meaningful drawings to do as they progressed. Since he had a nucleus of very top professionals, we were able to learn and develop very quickly. After a year, I was drafted into the Army and spent the next five years in the infantry, doing very little art work. Khaki was the "in" color in men's clothes.

When I got back from overseas and separated, I decided to free lance. So I went to the Art Students League night school to study with the revered Howard Trafton. He taught a very exciting course in drawing and design and acquainted his students with fine art; many for the first time. His classes emphasized the values of sound draftsmanship and how it could be applied to all the facets of art. Through the years I returned to Trafton's class

for a few months at a time and always felt my interest in drawing and painting quickened.

I was now a specialist in men's fashion; and, as my uncle predicted, it was lucrative. But it was more than that; I saw that some of the most honored and admired people in the entire commercial field were fashion artists. The reason was superb draftsmenship. Fashion drawing was undergoing a dynamic change from a sort of cliche representation by formula to exciting, spontaneous and dramatic graphic art, which presented the fashion picture in new and very contemporary terms. This era was sparked by artists like Carl Erickson, Rene Bouche, Carl Wilson and Robert Goodman.

I began to evolve some very definite ideas as a result of all these influences. The central thought being that a fashion illustration was affected by certain key factors; newspaper reproduction, the delineation of merchandise from a graphic point of view and the presentation of a distinct fashion personality. I decided on drawing the figure basically in line with flat halftones or color added, but only **incidentally.** And with shadows and shading generally disregarded — or at least academically disregarded — but very **much** considered as design. I began to get calls from art directors who wanted drawings of people that were not strictly fashion drawings but did look chic and fashionable. Occasionally I got called upon to draw a specific personality. I discovered that I really loved to draw people. This led to an exciting new interest in drawing and painting portraits in all my spare time.

Since I lacked an academic foundation in painting, I decided not to worry about it, but to approach the canvas almost the way I would a fashion illustration. That is, basically drawing the subject in a brush line and carrying the painting forward from there. The look of a painting done this way satisfies me; and although I have experimented with other approaches, and try not to have too many preconceptions, I think that all the years of doing linear drawings, have convinced me that drawing with paint is the answer for me.

I try to let the spirit of the line remain untouched and untampered. I want it always to look like handwriting and to retain the verve of an observation put down when the hand and eye were **both** feeling the same sight.

This can't happen if you use your drawing only as a means of "fencing off" color.

I also go sparingly on elaborate backgrounds. Here, I like to **suggest,** again, with drawing. I find the canvas itself is pretty handsome stuff and I like it to show. Often, I put a tinted wash over the entire thing to set the stage for what's to come.

All of us are curious of course to see where our growth as artists will lead us. At the moment, I'm at the point I've just described — and I can't envision a day of heavy impasto wall-to-wall paint and elaborate story-telling background in my portraits.

I think I shall always hover where I do now with a primary interest in likeness, gesture, design and lively color. And above all, I want my canvases to have **zest.** With me, this will always stem primarily from drawing.

FATHER LLOYD — oil on canvas 30 x 40
This was a refreshing subject — an
Episcopal priest who sat in full regalia.
I tried to keep the portrait away from
the formality suggested by his
appearance.

C. C. BEALL — 30 x 40 oil on canvas
The sitter, a famous illustrator, was 81
years old, witty, dynamic and really
inspiring to paint.

DORA — 30 x 40 oil on canvas
I tried in this painting to do justice to
a distinguished looking woman who
projects great taste and a definite
point of view.

122

EILEEN — oil on canvas 30 x 40
This portrait of a lean chic woman was done on unprimed canvas, the neutral color of which I felt would hold the vivid colors of her dress together with the rest of the picture.

BARBARA — 30 x 40 oil on canvas
A portrait in basically two colors — gray and yellow.

ROSMINE — 26 x 30 oil on canvas
A portrait done in one sitting of a very vital, strong man.

NEIL — 30 x 40 oil on canvas
A one shot portrait of a fellow painter, placed on the canvas in an unusual way to make an interesting composition.

ANDREE — 26 x 30 oil on canvas
The canvas in the background was left largely untouched as was most of the drawing, emphasizing only the essentials.

NORMA — 36 x 72 oil on canvas
Portrait of my wife — this was my third attempt to capture her
(on canvas) and to include other elements that I thought important
— her clothes and enough of our home in the background to
suggest a milieu.

HUBBARD SLACKS — This is a unique account. The manufacturer
does not supply any specific merchandise — but leaves the
selection of material, style and color to me, since this is really an
institutional series. I do the ad in all its aspects, including layout,
design and illustration. The drawing is done with a black felt tip
marker. Acrylic color is used to paint in the figure (the background
is sometimes colored paper, cut and pasted.) I thought that by
using a flat poster-like approach, I could achieve maximum
impact on the magazine page. ▼

ONE OF THE WORLD'S GREATEST

SHAVE LATHERS IS NOT FOR SALE

But, it is yours as a bonus with any Braggi purchase at Harry's Bar ™

during the next 10 days! Yes, you get 2 months-worth of keen, clean, unscratched shaving

with this rich, creamy foam when you treat yourself to any of the 22 Braggi

grooming essentials. All conceived and created by Charles Revson, the man behind Revlon.

Among the favorites: Braggi cologne, 7.50. Pre-Blade Beard Softener, 3.50.

After-Shave Balm, $5. Braggi Face Bronzer, $5. Harry's Bar ™,

Street Floor, New York and all stores.

Bloomingdale's

SAKS 5TH AVENUE — These black and white drawings for Saks 5th Avenue were done with charcoal on bond paper. Lamp black watercolor was used for the wash tones. In each case along with showing specific merchandise, I had to give the impression of different age groups and types of personalities. The backgrounds were drawn originally on the streets and later combined with the figure in the studio.

NORTH LIGHT
...a source book for artists

The rusty side of painter Porter

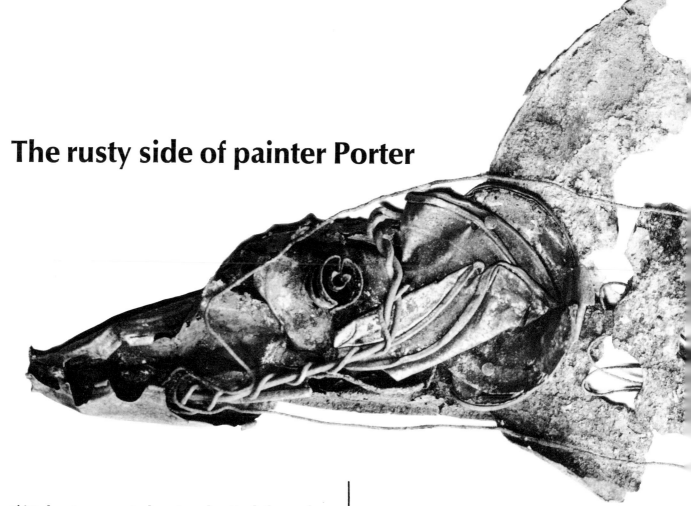

If it's beat-up, rusted-out and rotted-through, George Porter will gratefully receive any metal droppings you care to deposit at his studio door.

After a long career (still going strong) of illustration and painting, this Florida born artist is finding himself artistically reborn through sculpture.

I HAVE A SUSPICION that most artists who eventually turn to sculpture do it through some fluke event that comes unexpectedly. Surely it happened that way to me.

A couple of years back, I was tidying up around an old stone wall on my property when I unearthed a batch of corroded metal bits and pieces of intriguing shape and texture. Included was an unusual old wrought iron hinge and some Indian flints. I was fascinated with my find — the colors and shapes — so I brought them into the studio and piled them with the rest of my "art collection" of old bottles, stones, driftwood, etc. They went untouched for some weeks while I busied myself with commercial deadlines.

But something had happened in my head — I was hooked! My whole artistic direction took a 90° turn. I was now the victim of an all-consuming itch called *sculpture*. Perhaps *assemblage* is a more accurate term for what I now do, considering the fact that hundreds of pieces of metal sometimes go into a single one of my figures. They are pounded, torn or twisted and are held together with wire or nails or cold solder — plus *determination*.

My passion has long been painting, not wholly representational — more toward abstract expressionism. Just recently I completed twenty paintings for the Norcross Company, an international promotion, paintings for the Roure du Pont Co., a limited edition

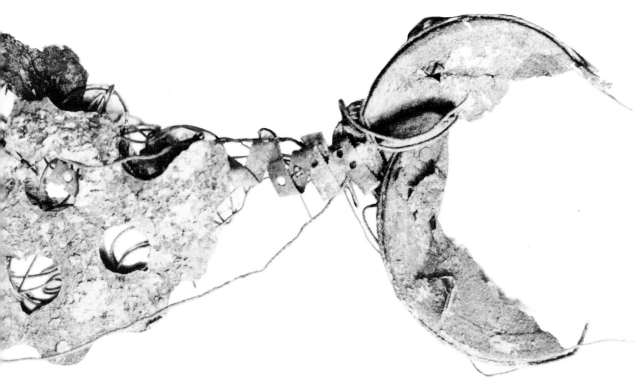

book, and several one-man shows. Most of my professional life has been spent in illustration, advertising, and books. My work has appeared in almost every major magazine here and abroad (live and deceased)! The urge now to do sculpture is new and exciting; it also affords a graphic quality that I never had realized in my painting or illustration.

In retrospect, my exposure to sculpture was extremely limited. In Sarasota Fla., my first year in the Ringling art school, we had access to one of the country's very fine sculptors. Again years later I studied abstract painting under Reuben Tam, trekking to the Brooklyn Museum Art School evenings. Next door were studios devoted to sculpture — but working in three dimension didn't even tempt me. My first years in New York were spent at the Phoenix Art Institute studying with such great illustrators as Thomas Fogarty, Sr. and Franklin Booth. I've wondered many times had I followed through with my original plan to attend the College of Fine Arts at Yale University, how different my life might have been. But I was lured by the glamour of magazine illustration, then at its height; I strove for more immediate results.

Many people have commented that I *draw* with metal. This is probably true, because many of the first things seemed static to me until I introduced wire — to define the figure and the action. Only then did I see the exciting possibilities of saying a lot without spelling it out. I've always admired those painters who have mastered the art of producing a picture with finesse and an economy of detail — letting the viewer fill in the missing parts. There are exceptions of course, when there is a specific problem to be dealt with or nostalgia is required. With the metals, one single piece can suggest something to me. With the decision to tackle an elephant and a rhino, the bulk of the animals immediately intimidated me. In the elephant I wanted movement; it's an animal not normally associated with action. He had to have the appearance of great size without simply using up all the metal in my studio — plus a feeling of fluidity. Once I began to nail down the first evidence of motion, even as one would start a sketch in life class, the rest of the figure simply grew — refinements came later. At times pieces were out of tune with the whole and were discarded.

Accomplishing motion automatically requires a knowledge of the muscles and skeleton. Certainly any figure in third dimension, even the most modern, requires a basic statement of fact — standing, running, lying down, etc. I've tried in almost every instance to incorporate the basic skeleton and go from there. The figures mounted on a flat board or plaster in relief were realized so much faster when the skeletal action was developed. The stand up figures, of course, required an armature describing the action. Given that from the start, all the odd pieces of metal could be used to advantage in creating the finished piece. I find it difficult to describe my fas-

The abstraction on the right was commissioned by Roure du Pont Co. I was given two bottles of perfume with instructions to sniff the fragrance and paint my reaction. To me it represented deep woods and exotic growth. And that is what I sought to capture.

The three pictures below are part of a card series I've done for the Norcross Company. Each depicts a pleasurable memory in a poetic way.

The boy-girl illustration is typical of what was in vogue in the 60's. This appeared in color in Good Housekeeping at that time.

Courtesy The Norcross Co.

130

cination! I'm certain, given a hunk of clay, I would never fashion anything as intriguing and meaningful as I can by taking these old pliable pieces and tearing off, bending and twisting and seeing them become a critical part of the figure — expressing even the personality.

Recently, I developed a strong desire to tangle with Don Quixote. My first thought was armor — metals — a natural. The more I considered it the less inclined I was to use metal for metal. How much more poignant the figure could be, especially in ruffles and lace of the day. The helmet and sword would follow.

The possibilities are limitless. Everytime I spot an especially interesting hunk of crushed and rusted metal, my imagination runs wild. My friends who had previously decided that the whole art business had affected my reason, are now hoarding pieces and presenting them to me with great fanfare, or they simply drop them at the door of the studio and run.

A project in mind now is a group of Nuns, European in flavor, with their fabulous habits. I can visualize the use of sweeping metals with the sharp edges describing the shapes of the headpiece and habit. As I said earlier, it is a large itch.

This past summer I spent days in a valley in Vermont hunting for materials to work with. I uncovered the remains of an original Model T Ford, a bonanza! Pieces of fenders, seatsprings, hood and all. Mind you, not for restoring, it was too ripe — just ripe enough for my use.

After three months of my first contact with this "new found art form", my wife insisted I have a tetanus shot. I did. Probably the reason I'm not lockjawed. This is hardly a dainty medium. Working with the metals seems to give me a new insight into my other work. Drawing and painting take on a new depth. After four or five days wrestling with pliers and hammers, it feels strange to pick up a brush and apply oil to canvas. The difference is refreshing.

THE COUNTRY DOCTOR

THE BULL FIGHTER

photos by Bill Noyes

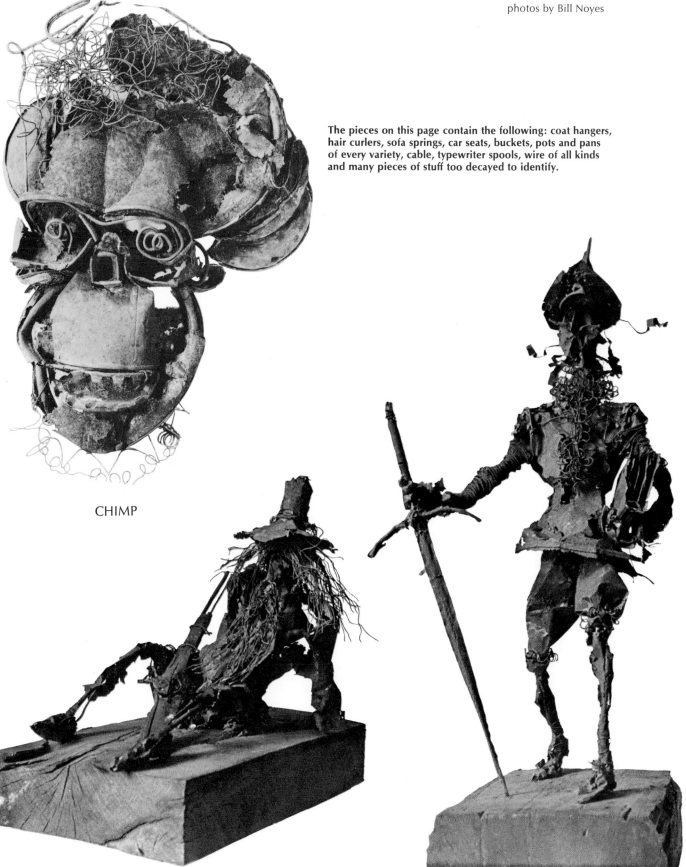

The pieces on this page contain the following: coat hangers, hair curlers, sofa springs, car seats, buckets, pots and pans of every variety, cable, typewriter spools, wire of all kinds and many pieces of stuff too decayed to identify.

CHIMP

RIP VAN WINKLE

DON QUIXOTE

Walt Reed: member of the family

Here, with his own private north light, is the welcomed newcomer.

In recent years, Walt's reputation as Illustration's foremost historian has become recognized. His knowledge of this subject is increasingly sought. He's especially active on the Sanford Low Collection of American Illustration for the New Britain Conn. Museum.

PICTURES HAVE FASCINATED ME for as long as I can remember. Not only is it a challenge making my own pictures, but the appreciation and study of the work of other artists have been a source of continuous pleasure and interest. While my appreciation includes approaches as diverse as those of Picasso, Wyeth, George Herriman's "Krazy Kat," Rembrandt, African masks, Japanese prints and calligraphy, I admit to a special interest and love for American Illustration.

While I was still an art student at Pratt Institute in Brooklyn, one of my teachers, Nicholas Riley, first introduced me to the wonderful world of Howard Pyle, founder of the Golden Age of American Illustration. As an art student, the magnificence of Pyle's drawings and compositions, as well as his concepts, impressed me tremendously. When not attending classes, I would spend my free time browsing in second-hand book stores where one could still readily find bound volumes of back issues of the old HARPER'S MONTHLY, SCRIBNER'S, McCLURE'S and CENTURY magazines which contained the work of Pyle, Edwin Austin Abbey, and many other great illustrators beginning back in the 1880's and continuing on through the turn of the century. I gradually began to acquire a large number of printed examples of their work which eventually threatened to crowd me out of my small YMCA room. Of course, at the same time, I was very much aware of the work being done by contemporary illustrators, then led by men like Dean Cornwell, Norman Rockwell, John LaGatta, Harvey Dunn, and Pruett Carter. As I studied their work, I began to recognize their styles and was able to identify virtually all of the illustrators who were or had been practitioners of any importance. I carefully clipped tear sheets of their work and filed them away alphabetically as part of my general art reference file. As time went by, this part of my file took over in volume and affection.

After art school, Pratt Institute and the New York-Phoenix School of Design, came marriage to an attractive young assistant to the picture editor of "This Week" magazine. There was an interlude of trying to get established as an illustrator and the frustration — and appreciation — of being supported mostly by my new wife. Then an opportunity came to go abroad as an overseas staff member for C.A.R.E. That agency, formed in the aftermath of World War II, was engaged in the huge relief effort in

Indian Street Musician

135

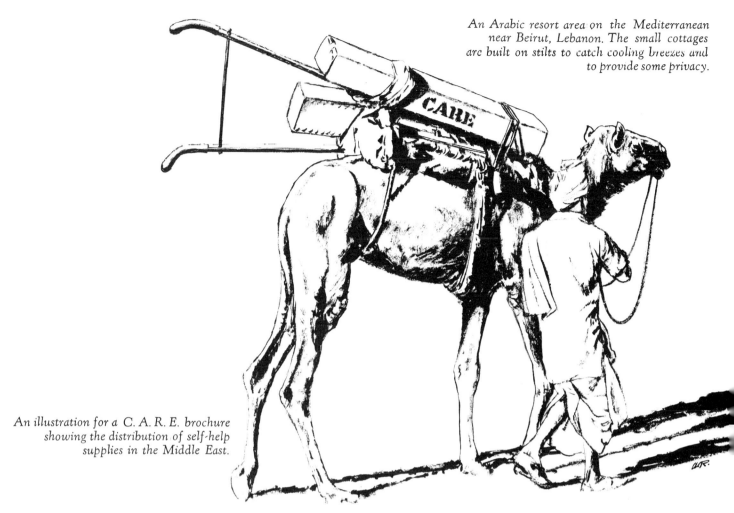

An Arabic resort area on the Mediterranean near Beirut, Lebanon. The small cottages are built on stilts to catch cooling breezes and to provide some privacy.

An illustration for a C. A. R. E. brochure showing the distribution of self-help supplies in the Middle East.

most of the countries of Europe and later into underdeveloped areas in all parts of the world. When I was offered the job opening in Czechoslovakia, seeing a new part of the world was too good an opportunity to pass by, so in 1948 my wife and I arrived in Prague and thereafter spent the next four years successively in Finland, the Middle East (based in Lebanon), Greece and Yugoslavia.

During our stay in Europe, there was a lot of hard work in supervising distribution of relief packages and commodities. There was also an opportunity to really absorb the feel of the countries, since we stayed in each one a relatively long period of time. I was fortunate, as well, to be able to record our travels through sketches and paintings.

In 1952 I returned to the New York home office of C.A.R.E. to become the Art Director for the parent organization. I remained for three years and then left to free lance in the book publishing field. In 1957 I joined the instruction staff of the Famous Artists School. Teaching others was as much an aid to improving my own skills as it was in helping others, and my free lance work became much stronger.

My affiliation with the Famous Artists School also provided a marvelous opportunity to know and work with a large number of professionals including the famous guiding faculty. It was a privilege to meet artists like the late Albert Dorne, founder of the School, Harold Von Schmidt, Norman Rockwell, Stevan Dohanos, Austin Briggs, Peter Helck, and Al Parker whose work I had followed and greatly admired.

The faculty member who influenced me most strongly was Harold Von Schmidt and he was kind enough to advise me about some of my professional assignments. As I learned more about his colorful career, it occurred to me that an interesting book should be written about him and his pictures.

Before long, the idea of doing a book about "Von's" illustrations began to take on a larger dimension, and I wondered if it would be possible to do a book on the whole history of that inspirational period of illustration. I realized that I was in a particularly advantageous position to undertake such a project, since I not only had much of the past material at hand but also had contact with so many of the living illustrators who were either affiliated

On a visit to the small settlement of Utsjoki at the northernmost point of Finland, I was impressed by the colorful clothing of the Laplanders. Among several paintings made there were portraits of these two Lapp ladies.

with the school or who lived in or near the town of Westport. Al Dorne was very enthusiastic about the idea, and it was he who got the project off the ground by introducing me to Jean Koefoed of Reinhold Publishing Company.

With the contract signed, the next five years were spent in the monumental job of obtaining and selecting the best examples of work out of a particular artist's entire career, tracking down the artists or relatives of deceased artists, obtaining permissions and then laying out the whole book in some order. The project began as a labor of love and remained so, even though it meant eliminating any other activities beyond my teaching at the school, thus sidetracking my own career in illustration.

Once that book was completed, there was still the story on Harold Von Schmidt to be done and that became my next project, just completed. The book, HAROLD VON SCHMIDT DRAWS AND PAINTS THE OLD WEST, will be published this fall by Northland Press of Flagstaff, Arizona. The book will also be made available to NORTH LIGHT Book Club members by special arrangement.

These projects led to writing other articles about art and artists for magazines, and eventually to a position as Associate Editor for the FAMOUS ARTISTS MAGAZINE.

When Bill Fletcher invited me to join the NORTH LIGHT staff, I was delighted to have the opportunity to use this combination of interests in art and writing even more fully. I look forward to the prospect of working with Editor Howard Munce and to help in the development of books which will impart their instruction and inspiration. We hope you will enjoy the results.

Studies of patients in a mental hospital. Without making any artistic comparisons with El Greco who is believed to have used patients from a nearby asylum for models in his religious paintings, I found that the stark reality of their conditions and their unaffected poses made powerful subject matter.

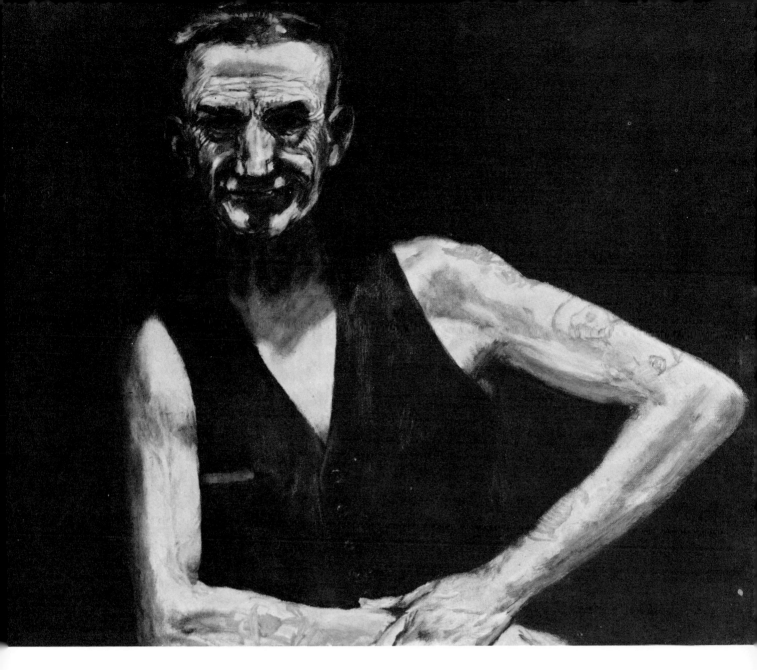

The accompanying illustrations were all done on location during my travels. Like many artists who take a camera along on vacation trips, I also took a lot of photos to be used for future reference. However, the photos remain packed away, never to be used. I believe that the physical and mental process of an hour's concentrated observation, drawing and painting of a subject, gives an artist far more knowledge about a place than simply clicking the shutter of a camera from a dozen different angles.

North Light

...a source book for artists

Joli

MINIATURE PAINTING is a very special world of its own. It demands exact draftsmanship. And it has never been affected by the modern art movement or fashionable "isms" to any noticeable extent.

Yet, miniatures have a very close, personal appeal. They can express a certain delicacy, combined with power, a strange combination — hard to duplicate in any other medium.

Perhaps miniature painting is at its most demanding and its best when executed on ivory. However, ivory has become increasingly difficult to obtain. Arthur Brown and Co. in New York is the remaining supplier I know of.

I usually start by finding an attractive antique frame or an old fashioned locket. This is an important first step, because frame and miniature pictures have such a oneness. Also such frames are sometimes hard to locate. The ivory is cut to fit the frame.

Ivory often comes with a highly polished surface. This should be roughed with an abrasive, such as finely ground pumice in a cloth sack so the watercolor will take. Pencil is never used for the drawing. It should be done with a brush and light grey wash.

It is important to use brushes especially designed for miniature work. A Sable Series 12, No. 5 brush is excellent. It has a wide base which holds the water, yet it tapers down to a few hairs.

Also, the Series 7, No. 5 brush is excellent for fast, broad backgrounds and for extremely delicate finishing touches.

Usually, I start a portrait with broad washes of watercolor. Then I work with a magnifying glass when finer details are needed.

It is necessary to use a palette of transparent colors, as the ivory should be permitted to glow through as much as possible.

This is the one I use:
Aureolin yellow
raw sienna
yellow ochre
burnt sienna
rose madder
alizarin crimson
viridian
cobalt blue
ultramarine blue
prussian blue

I avoid black, as I feel it kills a color scheme. White is not necessary as small changes are accomplished with a coarser dry brush and water. However, cuttle fish bone can also be used as a kind of eraser if preferred. This can be bought in pet shops.

After the first broad wash stage, I usually finish the portrait with small stipple dots of color, saving as much of the original start as possible.

A chamois skin is most helpful to keep dust off the ivory. This is the worst enemy of the miniature painter.

Gum arabic or oxgall can be used as tension breakers if the watercolor washes bead up and do not sink smoothly into the surface.

The ivory should be thumb tacked to a soft pine board at all times as it has a tendency to curl when a broad wash is laid on. If this happens — let it dry under a weight. Go gently, as sudden moves cause it to split.

Traditionally, a finished portrait was sealed in its frame with gold beaters skin. However, transparent tape is a good, albeit less romantic, substitute. Anything to keep out the devil, dust.

Ivory portraits should be kept away from extremes of temperature and direct sunlight. Ivory will contract with dryness and expand with heat and humidity. It is necessary to allow for this in fitting the ivory in its frame.

There seems to be an increasing interest now in miniature painting. This includes still life and landscapes, as well as portraits.

And there are at least two Miniature Societies I know of. They are: The Miniature Painters, Sculptors and Gravers Society of Washington, D.C. and the Miniature Art Society of New Jersey.

Good things come in small packages

Glenora Richards, once of New London, Ohio, is a full sized artist who thinks Small and achieves Big.

Her miniature work hangs in the National Collection of Fine Arts Smithsonian Institution, Philadelphia Museum of Fine Arts, Mattatuck Museum of Fine Arts and numerous Private Collections.

Janine

Awards

**National Association of Women Artists
(First Prize twice, Medal of Honor once)
American Society of Miniature Painters
Lavantia White Boardman Memorial Medal
Royal Society of Miniature Painters, Sculptors, and Engravers
Elizabeth Muhlhoffer Award
(Won three times, Honorable Mention once)
First Prize
Pennsylvania Society of Miniature Painters**

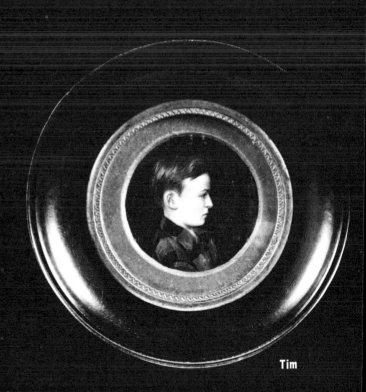

Tim

Oriental Girl

Dr. Sarah Richards

All paintings shown actual size.

Tim

Henry

Tim

Wally

Chin Hsueh Fong Tze

Note:
The paintings on this page are reproduced
actual size. They are all water color on
either paper or board.

■

144

NoRTH
LIGHT

...a source book for artists

one artist:
one subject:
endless variations...

Walter Du Bois Richards originally of Renfield, Ohio is many kinds of artist: a highly regarded illustrator, watercolorist and lithographer. His work hangs in seven museums and the White House.

His piece for NORTH LIGHT dwells only on the technique of lithography which as you will surmise, can snare an artist forever.

Wally Richards at work on the stone rigged to his improvised drawing table.

ONE OF THE MEDIUMS I most enjoy using is lithography. I feel an affinity for the rich blacks and silver greys as well as the strength latent in its depth of values and strong contrasts. The surface of a polished stone has a beautiful texture and is delightful to draw on. There are problems too. Stones are heavy: 18″ by 24″ weighs from 80 to 100 pounds. Drawings must be planned in reverse and very few changes can be made on the stone. Thumb prints, coughs or perspiration marks will print. Litho pencils are soft and points last only a few strokes. They are also expensive, costing up to 50¢ — and I use hundreds of pencils. Printing is a chore and costly but I feel it all worth the effort.

Litho stones are KELHEIM STONE and come in three grades: Blue (hard), Grey (medium) and Yellow (soft). These colors are very light being only the tint of the stone. They are a kind of limestone that was laid down in the sea eons ago by the settling of minute shelled creatures. The stone is found now only in quarries in Bavaria. The process was an early commercial printing method first used in the publishing of music. It was invented by Alois Senefelder in 1798. Senefelder's mother asked him to make a laundry list but he had no paper handy so he wrote it on a flat stone with a greasy ink he was using for something else. Then he wondered how this might print and after much experimenting, developed the method. The process involved the repellent action of grease and water. Commercial printing on stone later became obsolete for obvious reasons of size and weight. Stones are now used only for fine art purposes, mostly because of the wonderfully textured surface. Some art prints are made on zinc plates or by means of transfer paper. I prefer to work on the more responsive stone.

I first make a careful sketch of the subject on paper, then place a tissue over the sketch and make a tracing in outline. This is then turned over which reverses the sketch and is traced onto the stone after inserting a sheet of paper coated with a dry red powder called "Dragon's Blood" between the tissue and the stone (like a carbon paper). After the tracing is completed I block out the border and any areas I want left white with Gum Arabic solution. When this is dry (in moments) I start to "render". Some artists draw directly on the stone with no preliminary sketch but drawings do not always reverse well. Portraits wind up with hair partings on the wrong side or people appear to be left handed, lettering and numbers may turn out to be backwards or cars on the wrong side of the road.

This is my first litho of the lighthouse. The State Department exhibited it around the world.

Litho pencils have carbon-impregnated greasy leads (wax, soap and lampblack), and come in five grades. No. 5 is the hardest and lightest grade and No. 1 is the softest and blackest. The carbon is introduced into the lead to equal the grease content so that one can judge the values of the marks. It would be possible to draw with soap or butter or any grease which would then print black but it would be most difficult to manage or judge what was being done. I use litho pencils chiefly, but stick crayons come in the same grades plus "0" and "00" which are very soft. Also Tusche, which is a greasy ink, can be painted and washed on a stone and tones can be rubbed on with a silk cloth which has been wiped on a stick of rubbing ink. Gum Arabic crystals dissolved in water can be painted over sections (like a "frisket" or stencil) and after drying can be worked over with crayon, pencils or rubbing ink. This protects the surface. Once these things are put on the stone there is no erasing and greasy thumb prints or a good sneeze can spoil everything. The crayon or Tusche can be scratched off with a sharp knife or razor blade but this spoils the surface and one cannot work over the scratches. It is possible to laboriously stipple a section with a lithographer's needle to re-create the surface and work over this. But it is so difficult that only minor areas can be chanced.

After the drawing is executed on the stone, it is etched. This is not the usual "etching out" but simply a fixing of the grease in the stone. Then the crayon is washed off the stone with turpentine so that the faintest indication of the drawing can be seen. Slowly . . . keeping the stone constantly wet . . . the drawing is brought back by the ink charged roller until the drawing is back to the original value or even a bit darker. The ink only takes to the places on the stone where the greasy crayon has been fixed and each tiny pore of this *Kelheim* stone holds a tiny drop of water to protect it from the ink. If the stone should be inked dry, the ink would take everywhere and the stone ruined. Once the stone is inked a damp piece of high quality rag paper is carefully laid over the stone and both run through a scraper press that transfers the ink from the stone to the paper. Usually prints are dried between blotters under weight. Many proofs can be made, the most I have done of one print was 500, but I suppose thousands could be made if carefully printed. The printing is done manually print by print with much care. However, most printmakers limit their editions.

I have made my own proofs but I prefer to have a professional printer do them. The most accomplished person

Cont.

MY INTEREST IN GREENS LEDGE LIGHT began twenty years ago. I had been on my first sketching trip to Europe and returned less enthused than I had expected. I thought of all the generations of artists that had made skeches and paintings of the same subjects in all possible manners and I felt like just another of the endless line of artists doing the same thing. It gave me a feeling of guilt.

After I returned home I happened to go to nearby Roton Point. It was a beautifully clear day and the slanting rays of a setting sun made a simple and dramatic subject of the lighthouse and for the first time in a long while I felt that here was something that was "American" and that I really *wanted* to do. That impression has remained with me ever since.

Subsequently, I bought a boat and sailed and fished and sketched around the light. I discovered it ever-changing in its moods, its strong simple design and its symbolic meaning for myself and others who used it to locate the harbor when far out on Long Island Sound. I know lighthouses like red barns are passé as subject matter but I feel this one is special for me.

The light was built in 1902. A severe hurricane cracked the base so that from certain angles it leans slightly but I always draw it straight. Recently it was to be torn down but happily, local effort has had it designated a national landmark and so it will remain. The windows are boarded up, the flag no longer flies and no personnel with their boats man the light. But I will continue to draw and paint it with the activity as I remember it.

In this version I used the gulls against a light sky with a more linear approach.

Blackfish Passing Greens Ledge Light 1910   Walter DuBois Richards

Here is an effort to get the wild feeling and assorted shapes observed one day.

My son, myself and our bass boat. This was done from memory.

I know is Burr Miller of 20 West 22nd Street, New York, N.Y. who has followed in his famous father's footsteps by carrying on this exacting craft.

After the edition is "pulled", the drawing is ground off the stone and thus the print is cancelled. The stone can be used again after resurfacing until it gets too thin to withstand the pressure of the press. Stones are resurfaced or grained by rubbing and revolving the faces of two stones against each other with water and an abrasive

(flint) between. Several degrees of texture or grain can be made as desired.

Since the stone is impractical to take out to the field, I make my final draft from field trip notes using the same methods of research and sketching employed by artists generally. I simply try to enjoy myself in doing my lithographs while expressing myself in my own way, and I don't worry much about what has been done by artists before me.

Sandpiper passing Greens Ledge Light #13   Walter DuBois Richards
13/35

This is a different view of the boat on the opposite page.

This reproduction is the actual size of the print.
It shows an end view of the rock base.

"Off Five Mile River" 3⁄60   Walter DuBois Richards

"Greens Ledge Light" 3⁄50   Walter DuBois Richards

day that suggested a Japanese print. The boats were forming for a race.

This visiting schooner passing the light made an appealing subject. I subsequently used it several times. The print is reproduced actual size.

"Blackfish II passing Queens Ledge" 17/50   Walter DuBois Richards

A stormy and moody day. The lighthouse with its cloud mantle was dramatically intriguing.

Fog and rain around the light caused a variety of effects — always a little different. I painted it a number of times, but this is the only litho, so far.

A very breezy October day — the title is "25 Knots At Greens Ledge."

north light ®

a source book for artists

the painterly evolution of
ALEXANDER ROSS

Alex Ross of Dunfermline, Scotland via Wilkinsburg, Pa. turned out 130 covers for Good Housekeeping alone!

His illustrations were in demand from all the big books through the lush years following World War II.

Then the magazine world and his world changed.

Ross' energies and interests are devoted mostly now to brilliantly colored gallery paintings which he executes with a very personal dash and verve.

His work is represented by the Joe DeMers Gallery on Hilton Head Island, S.C., the Collectors Gallery in Nashville, Tenn. and the Eric Galleries in New York City.

Morning Becomes Ecstasy

For the better part of my life I have been working at the making of art.

In that span I have sought to feed my mind with facts, ideas, knowledge, information and original thoughts — always for the single purpose of being better able to express myself.

It's very satisfying to look back on one's life and be glad in the knowledge that the course chosen was the right one. The years when I was an illustrator were rewarding and stimulating and I have pleasant memories of being a happy, hard working part of those exciting days.

In spite of the years of struggle to teach myself, drawing and painting have never been a chore for me. The fact that I was not able to attend an accredited art school may have delayed my growth — but that may also have been a disguised asset. If one is armed with some talent and boundless desire he can learn and progress through art books and endless practice. There is no comparison between today's books and the meager lot available in the 30's when I was scouring the library.

Obviously nothing takes the place of personal instruction from a respected teacher.

In the beginning I made hundreds of bad drawings, but happily I had good friends and loving relatives who thought they were excellent. Their praise gave me the encouragement I needed.

Like most young artists aspiring to be famous illustrators, I was interested in drawing the human form and capturing facial expressions, two important requisites if one ever expected to be given commercial assignments. So, I worked harder in this direction than any other.

It was about this time that I began to be aware of a disturbing fact. There seemed to be considerable sameness to much of the illustration of the day. The monotony of it bothered me to such an extent that I made a promise to myself that, should I ever "make the scene", I would make every effort to introduce into my own work an inventiveness which was so lacking in much of the published work in the early 40's.

Eventually I made it as an illustrator and soon found myself in a position to explore. Through the good graces and the confidence of some of the ranking art editors of the day, my penchant for new forms of visual concepts and expressions where given a green light. I still am awed at the freedom I was given to think creatively in an atmosphere that was so closely controlled by editorial policy and by headstrong art editors, with very definite ideas of their own.

Although growth as an artist continued over the years, eventually thoughts about directions other than illustration began to fill my mind. As the market for magazine illustration declined and photography rose in popularity, I began to make overtures in what I hoped would be a new future for myself in Fine Art.

The decision to separate myself from this highly remunerative field was not easy, especially so when I discovered an unknown painter's prices could not begin to match those of an established illustrator. But the challenge was there, and I believed that only in this direction could I fully express myself. More important, what direction was I to go in — what in the world was I to depict?

I've always had a fascination with that aspect of art which stressed non-conformity with nature. I hasten to add that I have a deep love of nature and its origins, but when I am confronted by a painting of meticulous realism by one of my contemporaries, I'm awed by its skill but unfulfilled by its content. I find no real challenge there for me — the mystery is gone.

Challenge is an unknown rocky road, strewn with obstacles and dead ends. But once overcome, what a feeling of accomplishment! In my own case I feel, not only justified but freely uninhibited when I alter the natural contours and characteristic form of an object. And if by doing so, I benefit composition, structure and esthetic value, I have achieved something.

Of course extreme alteration of an object's natural form transforms it to abstraction and loss of identity. I avoid this, because here again, I believe there is more challenge in the objective than the non-objective. In my opinion, the distinguished painter Julian Levi is a fine example of an artist who manages to accomplish this beautifully. His sense of the abstract never quite loses itself in complete non-objectivity.

Perhaps more important to me now than my thoughts concerning the alteration of form, are those which are concerned with the alteration of light and color on form. In recent years I have changed my thinking about light and color radically. I once had a block which my inventive bent could not cope with, but now I feel I have fashioned a new direction for myself. Specifically, it consists in the deliberate sacrifice of certain contours of forms when these same forms overlap or come in contact with other forms, similar or dissimilar. This applys too, when their respective values are the same or nearly so. They can be in bright light or deep shadow. In the case of the human form, this makes for a reasonable sacrifice of familiar contours in the interest of focusing more attention on an overall abstract pattern.

My color too, has undergone drastic change. Several years ago, I discovered in one of my paintings an area that struck me as particularly pleasant. It was quite high key in value, bright in color and cheerful, with a minimum of middle-to-dark accenting values.

In analyzing my feeling about it, I conclude that my sudden interest must have stemmed from the fact that the majority of paintings I encounter were far deeper in overall value. They concentrated heavily, for the most part, on middle and deep values.

I made up my mind at that point that here was a worthy direction for me to pursue. That became the beginning of a new phase in my work. For me, it is an exciting personal break-through and whether or not it is correctly labelled *inventive realism*, it is currently *my* kind of realism and for better or worse I have invented it for myself. I'm looking forward to the new and undiscovered directions it will lead me to.

Family Portrait

An early work for the Saturday Evening Post (1947) which perhaps constituted my first break with traditionally accepted illustration. Its appearance led to the first article about my work in the American Artist Magazine.

The Key

This illustration was done for McCall's. My plan was to introduce to the reader the main ingredients of the plot in a simply designed picture, rather than an isolated situation from the story which, in so many cases, turned out to be just another lovers' "clinch".

Blandings Builds His Dreamhouse

Again, a further example of the use of story background material incorporated in a provocative situation to help convey the preoccupation of the husband concerned with his building plans.

Flower Paintings

In these studies of flowers, or flowerscapes, on which I have been focusing a great deal of my time recently, I am attempting a departure from traditionally accepted concepts in flower painting by introducing a feeling of nature untouched, or perhaps a better way to describe it, as an effort to capture the essence of floral forms through some rather unorthodox interpretation.

Glow of Summer

I am often asked why I have changed my style so drastically. My illustrations were produced for the sole purpose of portraying an author's thoughts, so that hopefully, the visual teases would entice one into reading the story. That's what illustration is all about.

On the other hand, when a picture becomes an end in itself, it is no longer something that is incomplete without an identifying caption.

So today I find myself concerned with my own thoughts on what art is all about, and have moved steadily away from the kind of academic realism that was so prevalent in illustration in the past, and is still, to some degree, today.

I think this painting in oil, of a mother and child with its emphasis on abstraction through the use of fused values both in light and shadow, helps illustrate the extent of the change that has taken place in my viewpoint and style.

This is an example of my work at a time when I was beginning to feel that I had just about completed my career as an illustrator and was ready to go on to broader things. My evolution towards painting had begun.

Reflections

What I am looking for so often, is the presence of the abstract that is inherent in so many forms and shapes that are familiar to all of us. In this study of water and boats, I concentrated on the abstract aspects rather than the purely representational. Further loss of identity could have been ventured, particularly in the boat shapes, but I felt a restraining hand.

The beauty of nature is probably most appreciated in the contemplation, or study of flowers, and I am not trying to improve on an already perfect phenomenon. Realizing the impossibility of capturing all or part of a flower's mangnificence through paint has turned my mind to thoughts, perhaps metaphysical in their near abstraction, on how to catch a mystical something beyond the beauty our minds and eyes behold.

The Sisters

A study of flowers incorporating nude figures. The subtlety of the figures was intentional. In fact in this particular painting, I had the feeling I was reaching out into a white void, all the while trying to shape masses of almost incorporeal substance.

Bill Shields has worked the U.S.A. He was born in San Francisco — raised in San Antonio — studied in Chicago — succeeded in New York and landed in New England. And to avoid growing roots he has traveled and drawn around the world.

Among his honors are Gold Medals from the Los Angeles and N.Y. Society of Illustrators.

a look at the sharp pen & eye of big Bill Shields...

I would like to talk about drawing, initially, because it gives me great pleasure and has been of considerable importance to my career. Nothing has benefited me more than the many hours I have spent in life classes and in drawing on location. I have always drawn when I've had the chance, preferably in the company of other artists. The direct competition is healthy and stimulating — and often sobering. Drawing should be a totally intense experience to the point where, for *that time,* all else is nonexistent. Drawing should heighten every sense, making you fully aware of how you feel about a subject. That feeling should be evident in your drawing by the over-riding mood you have created by your lines, lack of lines, direction and intensity of the strokes. I have always avoided drawing with a pencil or any other material that smudges. I like the permanent feeling of having to make a sharp positive statement without the temptation to erase or change my drawing later.

About mood; this develops gradually through the years. Initially I strove for form and proportion to create likeness and to explain realistically what I saw in the subject. Through this approach I gradually gained confidence to the point, where now, I have added new dimensions to my work. I have been freed (through knowledge) to violate or bend rules of perspective or anatomy and to further exaggerate in the extreme. Since my work is still of a literal nature as well as impressionistic, it will always have recognizable subject matter, but *the mood* has emerged as the important feature. If I am drawing from life — either a figure or a landscape — I add to what I see before me something from my imagination or memory or by drawing the subject as a combination of shapes or parts of shapes that form a cohesive design. To me, this is the beginning of a totally personal approach to art and a proper break from the tyranny of nature. A personal approach — the thing that makes *you* uniquely *you* is what we should all strive for. I find it fascinating to allow my pen to flow, almost uncontrolled, over the paper surface. Of course, it really is controlled by an inner sense and knowledge of anatomy and design but almost subconsciously. The drawing on the right is such an example. I drew it while waiting for an idea to start this article. It is just a progression of shapes, allowing parts of one shape to suggest another thought or shape. I have dozens of such drawings some of which I'll use as a basis for future paintings. Most of them stem from personal experiences and are steps towards a deeper penetration into my inner self and talent.

⟫⟫⟫⟶

A general store near Houston done with a Flomaster pen. This is a good example of my early drawings when my lines and perspective were more or less straight.

A recent pen and ink drawing of the Tower of London. I was trying for a mood of mystery and forboding that is characteristic of the subject. By bending the perspective I was able to draw twice the number of buildings on a limited piece of paper.

A drawing of a Spanish courtyard. As usual, by distortion, I am able to show much more of the subject than normal. Many people have told me that I have a fish eye lens built into my head. This drawing was done with a BIC ballpoint pen. I find this a very sensitive instrument and an easy one to carry around.

A life study of a fellow student at the Art Students League. This painting was done with acrylics and in a bold manner. I feel that this was a very successful exercise and captures the feeling of the moment.

In presenting my drawings I have selected those that show a progression from the literal to the more imaginative. Note that the earlier drawings were made more or less by *rendering* the subject. Gradually you can see the exploration into a much more personal approach. I like to draw heads and bodies that help me say something about those human emotions I have observed at one time or another and have remained stored in my brain. I leave it to the viewer to fill in the blanks and hopefully add his personal interpretation. I want him to use his imagination and expand and stimulate his thought processes.

Actually I also still enjoy being literal on occasion, but I hope that, even then, a little of my feelings show through.

An extension of my drawings are my sculptured heads. I approach sculpture in precisely the same manner as drawing. I use a plaster type of material which allows me about 15 minutes to complete the form before the material sets up. I have no pre-conceived idea of what the head will be like, but as I squeeze and knead the material, faces and shapes appear before me. Here again I don't leave myself much latitude to change or

vacillate . . . the material demands that I move quickly and positively. After a day or so I can scrape or carve the surface to add texture and emphasize character. I guess all these heads are friends from my subconscious, and I am delighted to have the opportunity to bring them into being for others to enjoy (or wonder about). In sculpture as in drawing, I am working towards a multiplicity of images to create one design.

I am very happy that I am an artist and even more happy that I am an artist with a certain amount of imagination. The world abounds in subject matter that is waiting to be interpreted. It is rewarding fun to exaggerate the commonplace and to present it in a fresh and interesting manner. This way you can share with others, your feelings and your moods and perhaps become closer to them as human beings. As artists we have so many mediums and materials with which to work. It is fascinating to combine them in unorthodox ways. On the other hand a simple pen can have maximum muscle with the right touch. Art is really still wide open and it always will be. It awaits the contribution of each of us.

I feel that my drawings and paintings are taking on still another dimension in these, my most recent works. In most cases I have no pre-conceived idea of what the faces will become — but while kneading the plaster — they just appear before me. When the plaster has set up, I can carve them, thus giving them the appearance of stone. This is a medium I have just begun to explore.

Photos by Alex Maurizio

163

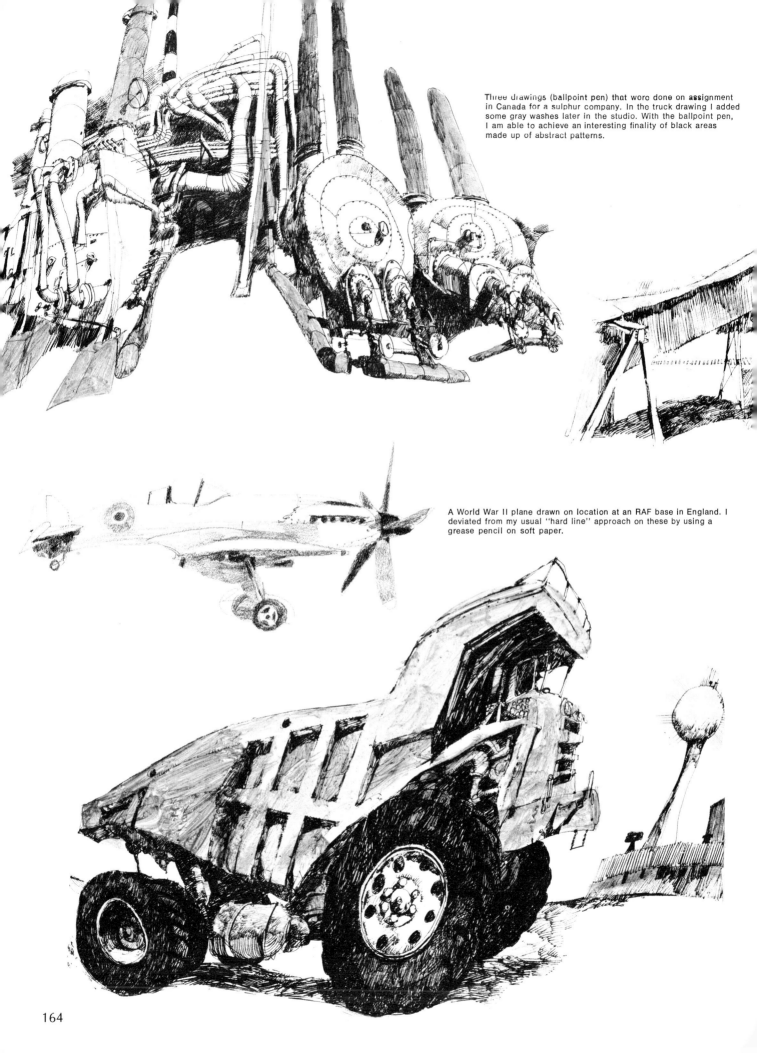

Three drawings (ballpoint pen) that were done on assignment in Canada for a sulphur company. In the truck drawing I added some gray washes later in the studio. With the ballpoint pen, I am able to achieve an interesting finality of black areas made up of abstract patterns.

A World War II plane drawn on location at an RAF base in England. I deviated from my usual "hard line" approach on these by using a grease pencil on soft paper.

These are faces of people on the cruise boat down the Rhine River. The faces unconsciously flow, one into another and somehow emerge into an overall pattern. This drawing was done with a Speedball pen and ink. I feel that this is the approach to drawing that I am now involved in and one that is most satisfying to my artistic sense.

Studio 2
...the art spirit at work

Bert Dodson
BORN: El Paso, Texas
STUDIED: Arizona State
School of Visual Arts, N.Y.

Privacy, quiet and solitude are a few of the states prized and sought after by most artists.

Many couldn't survive their lack.

There are others however, who are not only not disturbed by sharing studio space — they welcome kindred cronies nearby.

That's how Workshops come into being.

The following pages tell the story of one such group: STUDIO II. It occupies the loft of an old factory and is made up of six serious painters who met as instructors in the early days of the Famous Artists School.

I think their joint aims are brave and enviable ones. And they are told here not only because they are appropriate to such a publication as NORTH LIGHT but also because they might cause others to get together in communities across the country.

H.M.

Studio II sits on top of a plastic factory.
Downstairs everything comes out acrylic or polymer or lucite. Precision-smooth and odorless. But not upstairs. Upstairs gives off the smell of that most romantic of mediums, oil paint. It's one of the things I like about Studio II. There is a deliberate disregard for "relevance" here. Everywhere else I'm pressured to "speed things up", adapt to new technology and cope with accelerating change. Not at Studio II. In this group of artists one can sense an out-of-fashion connection of art with beauty, a concern for craft and draftmanship, and an unabashed appetite for things romantic.

I see Studio II, both the group and the space as a marvelous anachronism. It runs against the current conceptual hard-edge, colossal scale, multi-media grain of the contemporary scene. Its forms are on a human scale. Its edges are softer and its surfaces more tactile. It's above all, a place where one can get a firm grip on fantasy.

Death of a Spiritualist
8" x 15" Terra Cotta

I did this bas-relief after hearing the strange story of Mary Baker Eddy having been buried with her telephone.
On these pieces I draw with my thumbs, pound with my fists and incise with anything from ice picks to toothpicks. The terra cotta is then baked.

Ann E. Toulmin-Rothe
BORN: Hudson, N.Y.
STUDIED: Boston University
San Francisco Art Institute

It began in a bar on Main Street; the idea of forming a studio and a school. To be the only woman present in a bar with five men artists is an unusual predicament, at best. Granted it was best; those fine guys and me.

After the studio space was acquired and the school materialized, we found we communicated best when painting together. Actual words came later, after the working. During the working, we were more concerned with images.

Thursday was the best day. Four of us working from the same model. Chip is teaching next door, a class in landscape. Students peer in and watch us battle with subject, and with the same problems they have. The light changes. Noon. Lunch, wine, conversation. It becomes magic and untranslatable.

I see things more through the spirit than the eye. It is my view and my contribution. Sometimes, I make coffee. More wine. The talk gets richer. Hopper in Paris, Casals' cello, Last Tango in Paris, travel in Italy and always reminisces of our Gene Holbrook now living and painting in Mallorca.

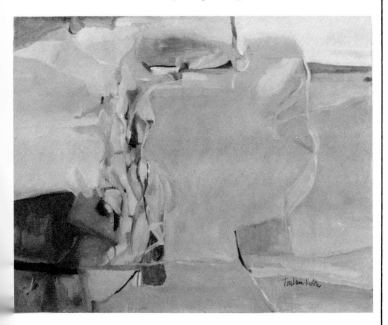

Variation on Rose Theme
50″ x 40″ oil

started a small fairly realistic painting of roses in a vase in the afternoon sunlight. On completion I found the stems n interesting linear problem and, using the basic design of ny life picture, began to explore it more abstractly.

Charles Reid
BORN: Cambridge, N.Y.
STUDIED: Art Students League

Studio II is a good place to paint and a good place to be. The light on a cloudy overcast day is soft and delicate. When the sun shines, light flows in, filling the studio with sharp contrasts and beautiful color. I guess it's the light that I love most here. I'm a "paint what I see" type and I can always find something beautiful to paint whether it's a bowl of wild flowers or a beer can bathed in sunlight.

Certainly I could ask no more of a studio, yet here there is more. There are good people — people I like very much — people I like to work with.

There is a special feeling among us and right now I like the way the sunlight is raking across the table in front of me making a beautiful, glowing object out of an empty Maxwell House coffee can.

Thursday Morning
50″ x 60″ oil

The painting was done over a 3 month period, working once a week. Each member of our group took a day off from painting to pose. The composition more or less happened. I depended on luck more than planning for the composition since I never had the whole group together at one time. This isn't a recommended procedure.

167

Robert C. Baxter
BORN: Plainfield, N.J.
STUDIED: Chouinard Art Institute

The place is flooded with light; the southern sun plants itself in yellow bars on the floor, coming through the windows and running liquid over the couch; the flowers on the table burst orange; wine glasses dazzle in the light. Other artists come and talk. Elena poses, gorgeous yellow hair, beautiful skin and breasts; there is music from "Cabaret", Joel Grey singing.
There is space and air and four artists painting and it is very nice to be here. It is whole and of itself; the right place, the right people, the right time; all together now, in a factory building almost 300 years old.

Walking Young Girl
Oil

Painting done from an initial observation: actual painting done in studio from memory, from which I work most creatively. The reality of the memory becomes distilled and clarified until the painting exists on its own.

Alfred C. Chadbourn
BORN: Smyrna, Turkey
STUDIED: Chouinard Art Institute
La Grande Chaumiere, Paris

One of the most rewarding informative aspects of our teaching sessions are the critiques held at the end of the class.
At this time the students are asked to hang their paintings on one of the big studio walls which gives them a chance to see their work in a total relation to the work being done around them. Our own paintings in progress are also in the room and many times they too get involved in the discussion. This sense of immediacy to the work being done brings us in a very close relationship to our students which I think they appreciate.
As artists we do have the same sort of problems in varying degrees and this awareness helps them relate these ideas to their own work.
We serve wine and cheese at these sessions and often the conversation strays to unrelated topics like what I saw in southern France last year or what someone thought of the recent show at the Whitney Museum. This too, helps in expanding and sharing our experiences which is all part of learning something more than what size brush to use for skies.

"Charcuterie"
46" x 52" oil

Interior of a delicatessen type of store in France. Done from sketches.

168

Ed Reinhardt

BORN: Brooklyn, N.Y.

STUDIED: Art Students League
Amagansett School of Art

Most of the problems I have as an artist are self imposed. Except for three, which seem to be universally applicable to all the artists I know: 1. The need for space in which to work, 2. the need for the exchange of ideas and opinions with other artists, 3. the need for money. The problems and goals inherent in the work process are set by me and can be solved only by me with only myself as judge of the solutions. Of the other three, Studio II provides the answer to two of them.

First of all it's nice to be able to feel the large studios are there for me when I need them. It's a little like the affluent feeling I have when a new stock of bronze sheets rest in my garage, or when the supplier delivers a new set of oxygen and acetylene cylinders.

As a kid I used to wander through art supply and hardware stores and somehow the full shelves seemed to hold the key to a lot of the mysteries of "making art". In those days, the prospect of having a studio with plenty of light, lots of space was also part of the fantasy. I could see myself, surrounded by partially finished sculpture and paintings, strangely content and most of all busy.

I've since learned there are no mysterious "keys" in the accoutrements but those early feelings are still there, every time I walk into the Studio it's with certain feelings of Deja-vue. I've been there. It's a place like I've worked in many times. My eye is comfortable looking around.

Exchanging thoughts and ideas is always stimulating — but difficult. The five other artists and the many students working in Studio II are all following their own paths. Our discussions while working or during our regular Thursday cooking and eating sessions run all the way from Alsace-Lorraine to Wounded Knee. For me a large part of communicating is listening.

For the third need, money, I've found no answer.

Warhorse
21"H-20"L Bronze

It's a horse with one leg gone — See title.

169

"Two nights a week we have an uninstructed sketch clas attended mostly by local professional illustrators — mos of whom haven't worked directly from the model sinc their art school days.
They're elated to escape the harshness of photograph that their commercial work often forces them to depen on. Many of them are also working in oil again afte many years absence.
Their enthusiasm is great to hear."

"The six of us also paint together from the same pos one night a week. This evening session has its own quie rewards. The mood is in sharp contrast to our dayligh work in the very same room."

"We're very fortunate in having an excellent choice o local models available to us.
We have a long list of interesting and paintable peopl to call upon — even some married professional model who pose together."

"One artistic stereotype none of us believe in is the starving-artist-in-the-garret.
On Thursdays we take turns preparing sumptuous lunches for the other five — and often a guest. The cooking is done right in the studio . . . and with the beautiful smells, noon is a long time coming.
Ann has kept track of all the menus and the recipes and has a cook book in the works.
Gene Holbrook, our traveling friend is at lower right."

Photos by Ed Reinhardt

"Our work is always on the walls for everyone's edification — mostly our own. But periodically we invite the public to view our things in a more formal way. Everything we show is for sale and it's also there to sell its authors to prospective students.
Most viewers and friends think our picture prices are too low. Perhaps so. But we'd rather they be "live" pictures in someone's house than stacked unseen in our racks. In the four weeks preceding Christmas we sold 38 paintings."

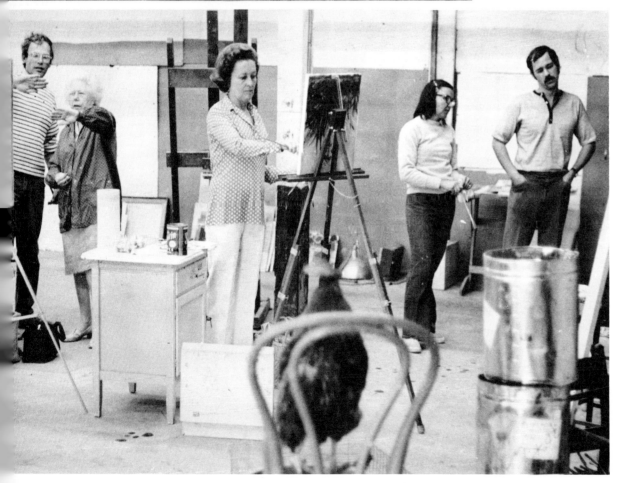

"One of the things that pleases us is the variety of students we attract. They are people of all ages — all kinds of previous training (or none) and every conceivable kind of taste and interest.
Nothing is more rewarding than to detect growth and improvement in a student — and to see each in their own way enjoy the happy purposeful atmosphere of this lovely beat-up place."

WHISKEY PAINTERS

WPA members are equipped with a 2 x 3½ inch vest pocket paint box. A cut-down brush with a jointed plastic handle fits inside.

OF AMERICA

A. E. Boedeker W.P.A.

Marc Moon W.P.A.

Don Stone W.P.A.

J. F. Faysash W.P.A.

MEET THE WORK OF TWELVE

MEMBERS OF ONE OF THE

MOST UNUSUAL ART ORGANIZATIONS

IN THE COUNTRY.

DON'T BE MISLED BY THEIR

JOLLY TITLE.

THEIR ORIGINS AND SERIOUS AIMS

ARE RECOUNTED ON THE

NEXT PAGE.

John Pellew W.P.A.

Ken Paul W.P.A.

Don Settle W.P.A.

Leroy Cross W.P.A.

L. R. Mong W.P.A.

Claude Croney W.P.A.

John Pike W.P.A.

Paul Strisik W.P.A.

174

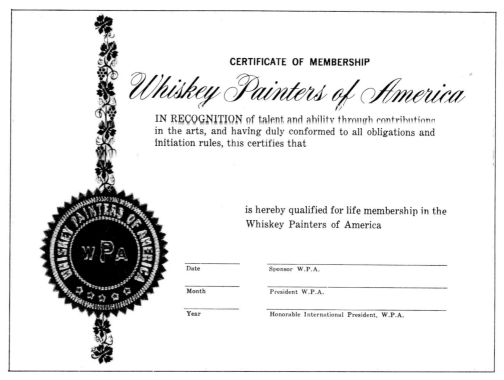

Club symbol and the coveted Certificate of Membership which confers right to use of the title W.P.A. after the artist's signature.

CERTIFICATE OF MEMBERSHIP

Whiskey Painters of America

IN RECOGNITION of talent and ability through contributions in the arts, and having duly conformed to all obligations and initiation rules, this certifies that

is hereby qualified for life membership in the Whiskey Painters of America

Date

Month

Year

Sponsor W.P.A.

President W.P.A.

Honorable International President, W.P.A.

Membership in this exclusive and unique organization is by invitation only, under the sponsorship of an active W.P.A. member.

Despite its title some of its most distinguished members are teetotallers. The W.P.A. roster now numbers some 90 artists distributed over the United States and South America.

In the mid 50's Joseph Ferriot, an Akron, Ohio industrial designer, and long time member of the Akron Society of Artists, formed the original small group of artists which later became the Whiskey Painters of America. He wanted somehow to make it possible for artists to paint and share their talents with friends wherever they congregated.

To carry out the idea, Joe designed a miniature water color palette complete with paints and a jointed brush and produced it in his own shop in Mogadore, Ohio. Watercolor paper blanks were cut and taped to expose an approximate 4 x 5 inch painting area. These blanks slipped nicely into the pocket together with the paint box. So equipped, an artist (W.P.A. that is) could sit down at a bar and draw and paint using the "liquids" thereon for his "mediums". — one "spirit" evoked

another and a club was born.

Ferriot quickly found that good artists do not necessarily believe in hard drinking—just soft colors and fun and friends. Formalities in W.P.A. are few but talent and fine craftsmanship are musts. Potential candidates must have shown in a juried show within three years prior to application for certification and paintings submitted for membership must be approved by the W.P.A. jury of selection.

As the W.P.A. membership grew and its activities increased, Ferriot asked the Akron Society of Artists to assume sponsorship.

In 1969, W.P.A. was reorganized with its former president named Honorable International President. Past president of the Akron Society of Artists, A. H. Don Settle, was elected to life tenure as president and secretary.

Although the organization is based on conviviality and its constitution and by-laws are couched in terms of humor, its members are all serious professionals who enjoy the relaxation of painting watercolors at miniature size for exchange with other members and for sale in their periodic exhibits.

In spite of their small size, the paint-

ings are not just "dashed off." As noted watercolorist John Pike, who is a charter member explains, "that would spoil everything. We work just as hard on the miniatures as on large scale watercolors and the compositions have to be planned just as carefully. It's just a matter of scaling down the size of brushes and paper."

A members' show last spring at the DeColores Gallery in Denver, Colorado, included over 600 miniature W.P.A. paintings and sales for the month totaled $21,-000.00.

The most recent show in September sponsored jointly by the Akron Art Institute, and the Akron Beacon Journal Charity Fund drew record crowds and was also highly successful.

Artists in other areas of the country who may experience some local apathy can similarly benefit from getting together in a joint effort.

Like everything else, art needs promotion. A good theme, purpose, or newsworthy idea for a show will do a lot to obtain the publicity that will create an audience . . . and sales. The Whiskey Painters have done it, and had a lot of fun in the process.

Walt Reed